Contemplative
KNITTING

Julie Cicora

Morehouse Publishing
NEW YORK

To Betty, Virginia, and Ethel,
my mother and grandmothers who taught me to knit.

Unless otherwise noted, the Scripture quotations contained herein are from the New Revised Standard Version Bible, copyright © 1989 by the Division of Christian Education of the National Council of Churches of Christ in the U.S.A. Used by permission. All rights reserved.

Morehouse Publishing, 19 East 34th Street, New York, NY 10016
Morehouse Publishing is an imprint of Church Publishing Incorporated.
www.churchpublishing.org

Cover design by Marc Whitaker, MTWdesign
Typeset by Rose Design

Library of Congress Cataloging-in-Publication Data
Names: Cicora, Julie, author.
Title: Contemplative knitting / Julie Cicora.
Identifiers: LCCN 2020045763 (print) | LCCN 2020045764 (ebook) | ISBN
    9781640652620 (paperback) | ISBN 9781640652637 (ebook)
Subjects: LCSH: Prayer--Christianity. | Knitters (Persons)--Religious life.
Classification: LCC BV215 .C55 2021 (print) | LCC BV215 (ebook) | DDC
    248--dc23
LC record available at https://lccn.loc.gov/2020045763
LC ebook record available at https://lccn.loc.gov/2020045764

CONTENTS

ACKNOWLEDGMENTS

Fifteen years ago, I decided to try and organize a spiritual knitting retreat. My first phone call was to Mary Ellen Arden whose name I found on our local knitting guild web page. She instantly said yes to the idea and helped me pull the first group together. The knitting retreat evolved into a knitting-through-Lent blog, more retreats, and now this book. I am grateful to all the knitters who have encouraged me in this process: Georgia Carney, the founder of Sew Green and the ardent sock knitter who attended the retreats and gave me pictures for this book. Pattie Blaine, for her contributions of pictures and support. Cindy Lill, Ginny Schindler, and Diane Doncaster, for being sources of consistent encouragement during the process.

I am especially grateful to my son, Chaz Goodman, for reading the first draft of the book cover to cover and giving me specific feedback, even though he has never knit a stitch in his life.

I am grateful to be a part of the Sticks and Cups knitting group from Utrecht, Netherlands. They are a helpful, caring, and supportive knitting community. It was this knitting group and the Fruity Knitting Podcast that kept me sane during the pandemic.

I want to thank Wendy Barrie at Church Publishing for suggesting the format of the book and for guiding me through the process.

A special thank you to my best friend and sister in ministry, The Rev. Dr. Cindy Rasmussen, who inspires me every day to walk the way of love.

INTRODUCTION

Rejoice always, pray without ceasing, give thanks in all circumstances; for this is the will of God in Christ Jesus for you.

—*1 Thessalonians 5:16–18*

We all know knitters who pray when they knit. They might be making a prayer shawl for a sick friend or knitting a tiny baby sweater for a new mother, perhaps asking God to be with the recipient of each knitted gift as they complete each stitch. The repetitive movements knitters make are calming and healing. Could knitting be a way of opening our hearts to God?

I struggled for years to maintain a regular private prayer practice. I found it difficult to sit still each day in the presence of God. It was so much harder than participating in public worship where there was singing, readings, and preaching. I found the order and content of the liturgy engaging, and there was a palpable sense of God's presence within the community of worshipers. Whenever I sat down by myself to pray the psalms or to say some intercessory prayers or to just sit in silence, my mind would start to race, the clock would slow to a crawl, and all I'd want to do is stop. I preferred reading books about praying rather than actually praying.

When I was in seminary studying to be a priest, a friend of mine gave me the book *Beginning to Pray* by Anthony Bloom. One of the stories he tells is about a woman who struggled with prayer. She felt an absence in the silence. The author suggests that she knit in silence before the face of God. After spending some time knitting in silence, she became aware of a presence in the silence. This made me wonder. Could knitting be a way into contemplative prayer? What makes knitting into prayer? Can our knitting habits inform our spiritual lives? This book is an exploration into the connection between knitting and prayer.

Contemplative Knitting is meant for knitters of all levels, and that includes beginners. It is not a book that will teach you how to knit or provide you with any specific patterns. Instead, it will outline some of the physical, emotional, and spiritual advantages of knitting. In part one we'll explore the history of the craft to discover how knitting has helped people stay connected and express love for others. What happens when we consider our own history of knitting? Who taught us how to knit? What was it like? For those of us who learned to knit before the advent of the internet, we had to find a teacher. Learning to knit was about forming a relationship with a patient and experienced knitter, a relationship that we treasured.

If you are considering learning how to knit or if you have just begun to learn, find someone with knitting experience who is open to sharing your knitting prayer practice. This kind of knitting is not about skill, it's about building a consistent practice that will help us deepen our relationship with God.

Anyone who knows how to knit can start a knitting prayer practice. Part two of the book will explain some ways of praying while knitting and give some suggestions on how to start. The spirituality of repetition is powerful. What is difficult is sustaining a prayer practice. We have to plan for the moments when we let go of our practice. There are some suggestions to help us get back on track.

How do we stay engaged with our practice? Part three can help us focus our prayerful knitting efforts around the liturgical year. Perhaps our knitting is something we need to use to pray ourselves through a grieving process or to help fulfill a charitable need in our community. Knitting can also be used as an evangelism tool to bring others closer to God.

Each section will offer some ways of reflecting on our knitting prayer practice. Our stash of yarn can help us learn about ourselves and identify obstacles that might keep us from a regular prayer practice. Reflection is a way to discover more about ourselves and our relationship with God. Adding a daily examen to our prayer practice is a crucial part of our spiritual journey.

This book explores how to use knitting as a tool to lead us into contemplative prayer, but we must be fully aware that private prayer is just one piece of our spiritual lives. We need to be part of a community that is dedicated to following in the way of Jesus. We are part of the body of Christ, and each of us has a role to play given the gifts that God has given us. Being in community helps us discover how we are a part of the body and encourages us to participate in God's mission.

Knitters know the importance of community and of gathering together for a time of fellowship where we can support and help one another grow in our faith. Public gathering as the beloved community to pray, worship, learn, and serve together helps form our spiritual lives alongside private prayer.

I love to knit. I love the feel of the yarn, the click of the needles, and the satisfaction of seeing the stitches accumulate. Knitting conjures up feelings of joy and gratitude that make me thankful for the knitters in my life, the knitters who taught me to knit, the knitters who offer insights into my spiritual life, and those who continue to support me in my faith journey. Maybe knitting is your gateway to contemplative prayer. Maybe, like the woman in Anthony Bloom's story, it will help to quiet your mind and open your heart to the presence of God. Let us begin.

Take Time to Reflect

Understanding Our Preferences, One Sleeve at a Time

But all things should be done decently and in order.

—*1 Corinthians 14:40*

I saw a man knitting at the airport. It was 4:15 a.m., and I had to look twice to be sure I wasn't half dreaming, but there he was. One solitary sleeve hung from his needles, the ribbed cuff swaying slightly as he dropped the right needle and used his entire hand to forcefully throw the yarn around the left, pulling it taut and then completing the stitch. He was riveted. His entire attention was focused on the project hanging from the needles.

My first thought was, "Why is he only knitting one sleeve?" Everyone knows that sleeves are knit together on straight needles so they are the same size with the same shaping.

Eventually, if we knit long enough, we develop our own sweater-knitting process. When I'm not knitting in the round, I start with the back. Then, I knit the front, the two sleeves at the same time, piece it together, finish the neck and weave in the ends. Sleeve knitting starts out fast. Cuffs are small and have far fewer stitches than the back or the front. However, as the length grows so does the width, and eventually one row on both sleeves becomes pretty time consuming. This man was going to town on one sleeve!

I didn't like watching him knit one sleeve because it was not my way. It is no wonder that our creativity and preferences are stifled when more experienced knitters insist on making us do it their way. Preferences are a way of expressing our identity.

I observed two right-handed parents trying to figure out how to show their left-handed daughter, Eliza, how to hold a crayon. She had developed her own way, which didn't look like anything they had learned in school. Forcing Eliza to change her grip was frustrating for both the parents and child. She even quit coloring for a few weeks.

Whenever I talk with people about prayer, they always want to know the "right" way to pray even though as adults they know there is no single "right" way to pray. Prayer is a way to know God, and how we decide to pray is a matter of preference. It needs to come from our deepest self. God knows who we are and expects nothing less.

One sleeve or two sleeves, throwing or picking, left hand or right hand, it doesn't really matter, we just need to do it.

Reflection Questions

1. How important is it to you to knit the "right" way?
2. How were you taught to pray?
3. What is the right way to pray for you?

PART ONE

KNITTING AND PRAYING

CHAPTER ONE

WHY KNIT?

The women in my family were knitters. At the tender age of four, I remember watching my grandmother knit, her metal needles clicking rhythmically, marking time until the smell of chocolate cookies wafting from the oven forced her out of her chair. I puzzled over how the ball of yarn at her side magically became the fabric on her needles. I watched in amazement as the thick wooly fabric transformed into a hat or mittens or a scarf or, even more unbelievably, a sweater. My grandmother had a superpower and I wanted it too.

When I was six, I was allowed to play with a tiny ball of yarn and some light blue plastic needles, but it wasn't until my third-grade teacher taught our entire class to knit that I began in earnest. Mrs. Powlaski decided that knitting would help her third-graders develop the small motor skills necessary for cursive writing. Although today my handwriting is barely legible, I have never really stopped knitting.

Everyone has a story about why they started knitting. Take the Wall Street trader who was recovering from a heart attack. Wallace was told by his doctor that he needed to do something calming. He racked his brain. He couldn't think of anything he liked to do that could be considered calming. Out of desperation, his wife suggested knitting. Wallace agreed to try it and joined her monthly knitting group. Within two months, he was knitting complex Aran sweaters with multiple cables and intricate stitch patterns, chatting happily with his wife's friends about the latest yarn reviews he found online.

The therapeutic benefits of knitting that Wallace discovered were already well known in knitting circles. Project Knitwell is an organization started by Carol Caraposa in 2010 to help mothers of hospitalized children relieve their stress through knitting and at the same time create a supportive community. Mothers experienced an immediate decrease in stress when they participated in the program. The results were so amazing that Project Knitwell began offering knitting programs for at-risk youth, cancer support groups, and caregivers. The knitting program complimented medical treatments and helped decrease stress levels and symptom of depression. Knitting was even found to delay memory loss and slow the onset of Alzheimer's.[1]

Stitchlinks[2] has been collecting data on the effects of therapeutic knitting since 2006. This organization offers a wealth of information about how to use knitting in conjunction with other medical treatments to promote well-being, particularly for those with long-term health conditions. *The Creativity Cure: How to Build Happiness with Your Own Two Hands* is a book written by two doctors that further explores how knitting and other artistic endeavors contribute to our well-being and happiness.[3] People knit because it is comforting, calming, and therapeutic.

Some of us knit for the pure joy of knitting. Just being exposed to the extensive variety of yarns found in even the smallest hole in the wall yarn store sparks joy. Ask any knitter how many hours they spend browsing and delighting in the vast array of colors, feeling the fibers from the softest baby alpaca to the smoothest bamboo baby yarn, and smelling the hint of lanolin on freshly spun wool. New fibers and colors are emerging constantly. The raw materials and ideas for this craft are limited

---

1. Leisure Arts and Lion Brand® Yarn Company, *Project Knitwell Presents the Comfort of Knitting* (Maumelle, AR: Leisure Arts, 2015).

2. Stitchlinks, accessed October 2, 2019, *http://www.stitchlinks.com/index.html.*

3. Carrie Baron and Alton Baron, *The Creativity Cure: How to Build Happiness with Your Own Two Hands* (New York: Scribner, 2013).

only by our imaginations, and countless patterns that guide us in making everything from a fairy tale cape to a simple scarf. There are patterns for mittens, hats, gloves, hand warmers, leg warmers, sweaters, shawls, and afghans, in all sizes, colors, and shapes. There are patterns available to make all the letters of the alphabet, an entire zoo, or even a sweater-like object that wraps around a tree. I recently saw an anatomically correct knitted skeleton, complete with organs and the circulatory system. The permutations of raw materials and patterns are endless.

Some people knit for practical reasons. Oma, my friend David's grandmother, knit so fast you could barely see the tips of her needles. Instead of throwing the yarn around the needle with her right hand (English knitting), she held the yarn in her left and with a slight movement each stitch seemed to wondrously appear. This style of knitting is called Continental or picking. When I met her, she was well into her seventies and a proficient knitter. There was no wasted motion. Oma would often tag along on family ski trips, and while her family was out on the slopes, she was knitting in the lodge. She would take over a table in the midst of skiers warming themselves near the fire and knit. Her needles in constant motion, her eyes darting around the room ever vigilant watching for her grandchildren coming in from the cold, her homemade kuchen and hot chocolate from her thermos at the ready. One frigid Saturday in February, Jen, David's youngest sister, confessed to Oma that she had forgotten her mittens. Jen was afraid to tell her father because she was always losing things. Oma silently reached inside of her Mary Poppins carpetbag and pulled out four double-pointed needles and a ball of chunky yarn. When her family returned to the lodge for a mid-morning break, there was Jen sporting her new mittens.

Marion, a friend from church, is a master knitter, a title conferred on expert knitters by the National Knitting Guild. She loves to knit the most intricate gifts, like a circular wedding ring shawl with yarn as fine as a spider's web. This pattern got its name because even though the shawl circumference is five to six feet, it's fine enough to be pulled through a wedding ring. Heirloom knitting requires copious amounts of time and love in order to transform gossamer silk into delicate stitches. Marion's daughter, Georgia, also an avid knitter, gives the gift of socks. Georgia always seems to have a pair of half-finished socks in her purse. I can tell Georgia's friends because they will pull people aside and yank up their pants to expose their new custom-made footwear.

Some people knit to proclaim their love and care for others. Shari, a knitting friend, told me her church knitting group creates a plethora of colorful, soft, cozy knitted clothing for the local schools, homeless shelters, and medical centers. One year they knit a total of 575 items that included: 319 hats sized infant to adult, chemo hats, 32 baby sweaters, 34 baby booties, 2 baby blankets, 64 scarves, 2 cowls, 36 adult slippers, and 86 pairs of mittens! Many of the people who benefited from this group's knitting have spent years wearing secondhand clothing scrounged from churches and shelters. For them, handmade knits were not just a warm item of clothing but an outward expression of love and time. Knitted garments are a tangible reminder that someone cares. The giver knits with no expectation of acknowledgment or thanks, creating a true gift.

Christopher's mother, Lorry, loved to knit. After she was diagnosed with Alzheimer's, she started knitting hats. Soon, she had a box full of multi-colored hats of all shapes and sizes. It was close to Christmas when Christopher paid a visit to St. Mark's and St. John's, an inner-city church in an impoverished neighborhood in Rochester, New York. The Wednesday before Christmas, neighbors were coming to the church for a healing liturgy and to pick up bags of food. Christopher watched as the parade of families expressed their gratitude to the volunteers for the opportunity to spend time in a warm, safe place where they could get some help feeding their families. He knew he had found a home for his mother's hats.

Lorry knit seventy hats every Christmas for the next few years until she couldn't knit anymore. Each Christmas, people from the neighborhood poured into the parish hall to peruse the table stacked with her handiwork. In January it was easy to spot unique knitted hats covering the heads of people walking down the street, shoveling the driveways, and getting into cars near the church. One memorable hat was made with a combination of bright orange chunky yarn paired with thin strands of hot pink mixed with lime green. An elderly woman, cane in one hand and a bag of food in the other, wore it proudly, stopping to tell people it was made especially for her. The community knew each other in the breaking of the bread and the wearing of the hats.

After Lorry died, her son kept the tradition of hat giving. He continues to ship a box of hats each year before Christmas to honor his mother.

I started knitting because my third-grade teacher thought it was a good idea, but I kept knitting for a variety of reasons. At first it was because I wanted the finished garment. I lusted after the big red chunky cardigan sweater with the little pockets, the soft pink pullover with the pirate sleeves made out of the finest cotton candy yarn, or whatever graced the cover of the newest knitting magazine. Later in life, I began to enjoy the process of knitting. It kept me company while I sat at Little League games, waited in doctors' offices, participated in conference call meetings, or watched boring weekend sports on TV. I could be happy anywhere—in the car, on the couch, in the airport—if I had some knitting. I never thought about knitting as a potential spiritual practice until I discovered the prayer shawl ministry.

Two women, Janet Severi Bristow and Victoria Galo, who met during the 1997 Women's Leadership Institute at The Hartford Seminary, started the prayer shawl ministry in 1998. The idea was born in their Applied Feminist Spirituality class and immediately took off. Today there are countless prayer shawl groups participating in this spiritual practice. They come from different religious traditions and knitting groups, and they are devoted to an assortment of ministries. People knit shawls for those suffering from cancer or other debilitating diseases, families of fallen soldiers, victims of domestic violence, first responders, and others. The shawls are their tangible sign of prayers for the recipients.

Knitting prayer shawls was the beginning of my experience of contemplative knitting as a spiritual practice. Soon, my practice of contemplative knitting expanded to knitting Advent blankets and Lenten cowls. I discovered that spiritual knitting could go beyond creating pieces to give away. The very act of knitting could become a way into a practice of contemplative prayer. I began to be intentional about praying with my knitting and soon realized that knitting could be a sacred activity. The repetitive motion of the yarn and the needles help me stay grounded while praying. It is a way to become immersed in scripture, prayer, and contemplation. This enjoyable, creative, therapeutic activity deepens my relationship with God.

Take Time to Reflect

Knitting and Prayer: A Simple Invitation

Create in me a clean heart, O God,
And put a new and right spirit within me.

—Psalm 51:10

Are you one of those knitters who follows a pattern exactly as it is written, or do you make modifications? Maybe you are one of those knitters who enjoys designing, and your house is full of swatches and stitch dictionaries. I've spent most of my knitting career following patterns to the letter even when they were wrong. It never occurred to me to change anything until I fell in love with a *Vogue* knitting magazine cover sweater. This one was a peplum-style sweater in an emerald shade of green. I ran to the local yarn store to buy the wool. They carried the yarn, but not the bright vibrant green shown on the magazine. I was devastated.

The store owner seemed puzzled at my disappointment. Why don't you make it in another color? She was stunned when I told her I always made the sweaters in the color pictured in the pattern. It was time to branch out and get creative, she told me. I bravely bought a gray-blue yarn that reminded me of a damp winter sky. The next decision was to make the sweater longer for my long torso. I began to read articles on alterations and design. Soon I was modifying patterns to suit my own needs and creativity. Patterns became basic templates, a starting point that could lead in a variety of directions. Cardigans could be turned into pullover sweaters, and mittens could become fingerless gloves.

Our prayer practice is a simple template—knit and pray. The design of the practice is up to us, and it can remain fluid. There is no set pattern with the practice, just an invitation to sit, knit, and pray. We have the freedom to create and modify what we do, where we sit, and how we pray. We can change our design to meet the needs of the moment. It turns out that the green sweater can be blue, the length can be longer, and a mistake in the cables can be repeated so it is no longer a mistake but a design enhancement.

There are knitting books that offer templates for all types of garments. The knitter creates a swatch, measures the stitches per inch, and then chooses a template. The knitter can choose what type of neck (crew neck, turtleneck, V-neck, boatneck), what type of sleeve (raglan, set-in, dropped), and a variety of other options. The book gives number of stitches, shaping instructions, and everything needed to create a sweater. I swatched some handspun yarn from Chile and created a V-neck vest using the template. I was free to start creating in my own way.

Prayer does not have to be done a certain way, using specific words at a specified time. Sometimes my morning prayer takes place in late afternoon, but it happens. I sit, I knit, and I pray. I ask God for help and mercy. My prayers are short and pithy, right to the point. That is how I pray, and it fits. When it doesn't, I'll change it.

Reflection Questions

1. Where do you fall on the modification scale?
2. When is modifying a pattern helpful?
3. What was the most significant modification you have made in your knitting life and in your spiritual life?

Changing Your Spiritual Awareness: Florida Knitting

For now we see in a mirror, dimly, but then we will see face to face. Now I know only in part; then I will know fully, even as I have been fully known.

—*1 Corinthians 13:12*

I visited a yarn store in southern Florida where the weather is hot and humid most of the year. As a knitter from the Northeast, I wondered what they could possibly be selling. The thought of wool or even the softest alpaca was stifling. Maybe they knit sweaters to wear in the frigid air-conditioned restaurants?

The store was open and airy. There was a long wooden table in one corner with twelve chairs, each with a different-colored crocheted cushion. A few women sat at the table knitting and laughing. Brightly colored yarns were everywhere, on the table, on shelves that ran the perimeter of the store, and in baskets strategically placed next to pattern kiosks. The woman behind the counter came out to greet me. She was wearing jeans and a bright white camisole underneath a navy-blue poncho that had been knit with ribbon-like yarn. Immediately the poncho went on my list to buy. It was gorgeous.

The inventory at this store was unique. There was only a small section of wool, baby alpaca, and other yarns I was used to seeing in the Northeast. They were for the women who wanted to knit gifts for their northern family members, the owner explained. The rest of the space was filled with cottons, silks, linens, ribbons, and beautiful blends. The colors were vibrant like tropical fruits, flowers, and fish. A woman was knitting a market bag out of red and green that looked like guava fruit. Here was another whole world of knitting.

How easy it is to become myopic. Our world can shrink as we go about our daily life and our perceptions narrow. When I worked as a chaplain in the hospital one summer, it seemed like everyone was sick. I remember going into the grocery store and being surprised that no one was walking around pushing an IV pole. It woke me back up to a world outside of the hospital where people were healthy. What we see on a daily basis can become our entire world. It's easy to think that everyone lives the way we live, thinks the way we think, and knits the things we knit. But what's outside our orbit?

The first step is to become aware of our orbit. After we leased an all-electric car, I learned quickly what my orbit was. I drove to work, to the grocery store, and back home all on a single charge. The car worked because my orbit was only a ten-mile radius. When I started tutoring at an inner-city school just outside my orbit, I discovered people living in extreme poverty. What I thought was totally familiar to me—the character of my city—was in fact just a small fraction of what actually existed out in the world.

Breaking out of the familiarity of our existence is important to our development as disciples. Once I discovered the people living in extreme poverty, I couldn't unsee them. My reality was altered, changing my level of awareness, helping me jettison my old perceptions and take action.

Now I knit with ribbon yarn and tutor kindergartens in the most challenged part of the city. I realize how important it is to go beyond my typical orbit and get out into the world. This is one result of a spiritual life: awareness is always changing.

Reflection Questions

1. How big is your orbit?
2. What false perceptions do you have?
3. How has prayer changed your level of awareness?

Finding Supportive Communities: Picking Up Stitches

Let the wise also hear and gain in learning, and the discerning acquire skill.

—Proverbs 1:5

Picking up stitches around a neckline is intimidating. I have to look up how to do this every time. I worry that I'm picking up too few stitches, creating an unsightly hole in the work, or too many stitches, which could turn into a ruffle.

Creating new live stitches that are perpendicular to finished stitches is the worst. The new stitches need to go in a different direction, and making this appear seamless is even more difficult. It can take multiple attempts to pick up stitches on the neck of a sweater and get them to look right. I correct my errors in each iteration until finally I'm knitting in the new direction.

A few years ago, I decided to work on my finishing skills. My Achilles heel became my growing edge. I bought a book, took an online class, and engaged a master knitter to coach me through the finishing process. It was the master knitter who helped me figure out what my blind spots were and how certain small mistakes, like stretching the hole where I was trying to pick up a stitch, added up to a messy final edge. It didn't take long for me to learn the techniques. I just had to decide to focus on learning and getting the coaching I needed. There is no substitute for a good teacher, and there is no substitute for a supportive community of students.

Lifelong learning is vital for our lives. We have to be willing to work on our skills, pick up where we left off, and go in a new direction. This is just part of the equation. We can't do this alone or we will stall out before we reach our potential. The best way to become a better knitter is with the help of a good teacher and supportive knitters.

Learning to become adept at prayer happens in our worshiping communities. There is a reason that Jesus said, "When two or three are gathered in my name, I am in the midst of them." We need the wisdom and energy that comes from being gathered together. Communal prayer is what propels us forward when we lack confidence. We may hear God calling us to go in a new direction, start a new ministry, or go deeper where we already are. Then the doubts rush in and plague us with thoughts about not being good enough. We worry about making mistakes. Communal worship draws us out of ourselves and gives us energy and purpose. The interaction with the community forms us into disciples.

Praying and knitting are both solitary activities as well as communal activities. We need both. Those of us who thrive on being with other people need to spend time in solitude in order to reflect on our own lives, to discern what God is doing. Those of us who enjoy the solitude of knitting and praying alone need to connect with communities. We need the wisdom and encouragement that comes from belonging to a community centered around the love of Christ. Together we are called to spread the love of God in the world. With the right teachers and support, we can pick up the stitches of our lives and continue to move forward.

Reflection Questions

1. Who are your knitting teachers?
2. What community will support you in your prayer practice?
3. What kind of teacher or class will help you continue to develop your spiritual life?

CHAPTER TWO
IN THE BEGINNING

"For it was you who formed my inward parts; you knit me together in my mother's womb" (Psalm 139:13). The Hebrew word translated as "knit" is *cakak*, meaning to cover, to make a covering, to entwine, to fence in, to protect.[1] The same word is used in the book of Job. "You clothed me with skin and flesh and knit [*cakak*] me together with bones and sinews" (Job 10:11). The word conjures the image of a creative God constructing our bodies, entwining the pieces together to form us into beings.

The English word *knit* works well in both examples because the process of knitting and the process of cell differentiation have a lot in common. The creation of knitted stitches is similar to the process of cell differentiation. Multiple knitted stitches are combined to form endless patterns that take on different forms with different functions. Some stitches become the cabled front of a sweater, and other stitches form the turn of a sock heel. Cells in the human body bind together to form tissues that then form organs with different functions. Some cells become cardiac muscles, while other cells bind together to form bones. The creative process in both instances stems from repetitive replication.

Today, the verb *to knit* has several meanings. The first meaning is the actual process of taking yarn, casting stitches onto one needle, and using a second needle to create more stitches that

---

1. Strong's Concordance 5526.

connect and make a knitted fabric. The definition includes hand and machine knitting. The second definition is to unite: "They are a close-knit family." Some dictionaries include "to join" as a definition of "to knit": "Time will knit the bones of her broken toe."

Contemplative prayer is a way to unite us with Christ. The process opens our heart and mind so that we can begin to be in the same mind as Christ Jesus (Philippians 2:5). The action of knitting, the joining together of yarn, can be an outward expression of our inward desire to be united with Christ. But like the bones, it takes time to knit broken pieces together. There may be parts of ourselves that need to be frogged (a knitters' term meaning "to rip it," "to tear out").

Just like learning to knit, learning to pray and develop a regular spiritual practice can be awkward, difficult, and frustrating. It can also be inspirational, rewarding, and transformative. The God who knit me together in my mother's womb knows each of us intimately and invites us into a deeper, more profound relationship. Just as we are made up of trillions of cells, and sweaters are made up of thousands of stitches, our relationship with God is made up of thousands of moments when we stop our frenetic activity, disconnect ourselves from the world, and fix our gaze on Jesus, our mediator and advocate, the pioneer and perfecter of our faith (Hebrews 12:2). A knitted garment takes hours to knit, and each stitch is necessary to the whole. Each moment we spend in prayer and contemplation is integral to our relationship with God.

Anyone who has ever knit a prayer shawl understands how we can become joined through the act of knitting. Even if we don't know who the shawl will be given to, we still pray for the recipient with each stitch. As a priest, I sometimes have the honor of delivering prayer shawls. One delivery stands out.

I was visiting patients on the oncology ward when I noticed a woman who sat propped up in her bed, a satin bed coat around her shoulders, blue veins visible through her skin. She was waiting, she told me, to hear the results of her last test, to see if her cancer had responded to the treatment. I held up a prayer shawl and asked her if she wanted it. I told her how each stitch is knit while saying a prayer for the recipient. Her blue-gray eyes filled with tears. Who made it? She asked. Someone who thought you might need it, I answered as I laid the shawl over her shoulders. Her bony hands gripped the edges together at her throat. She closed her eyes, sighed deeply, and whispered, "I can feel the prayers, every single one of them."

Our goal is to knit, to unite, to join, to entwine, to cover ourselves with the love of God. Intentional, prayerful knitting and contemplation is a sacred activity. With each prayerful stitch we focus our heart and mind on the Creator who knit us together and unites us in love.

Take Time to Reflect

Sacred Knitting: Discovering our Potential

Do not be conformed to this world, but be transformed by the renewing of your minds, so that you may discern what is the will of God—what is good and acceptable and perfect.

—*Romans 12:2*

When I was a child, my grandmother persuaded all of her friends who traveled to foreign countries to bring me back a doll. Now, my friends bring me yarn.

Whenever I receive yarn as a gift, I'm overwhelmed. It's wonderful to think that my friend thought about me on her vacation and then took to the time to find a yarn shop, pick out a skein, and bring it all the way home.

I feel that these skeins of yarn deserve special consideration. They are an outward sign of friendship. I sit with them, staring at them, touching them and visualizing their potential. One skein came in a brown envelope from Carol and Rich along with a beautiful note. They had just returned from their trip to climb Machu Picchu. The wool had come from sheep that live 14,000 feet above sea level in the Andes Mountains of Peru and was the color of pine needles, a deep, rich green. The skein sat on my desk for a few weeks forgotten. When I came across it again, I panicked. Here was a thoughtful gift that I hadn't yet acknowledged. I decided to make something immediately, take a picture, and send it to Carol and Rich. It was perfect for a hat.

Even though it was summer and close to eighty degrees, I cast on and started to knit a hat with a "V" cable pattern spaced evenly around the circumference. I prayed for the women of the Andes who tended the flocks of sheep and alpacas. I prayed for my friends, Carol and Rich. I gave thanks for people who take the time to give gifts that demonstrate that they know the receiver. How wonderful it is to be known.

I love wearing the hat. But yarn can change. This very hat can be ripped out, rolled back into a ball, and turned into something completely different. It could be wrist warmers; a short scarf to wrap once around the neck, the ends tucked into the collar of a coat; fingerless gloves; or paired with more wool yarn as part of a vest or sweater. The same raw materials can morph into so many different objects.

We are like yarn. We can go in myriad directions. As children of God we have enormous potential. If we are done being a hat, we can unravel and knit ourselves into something else. Being able to transform ourselves is a requirement in this fast-changing world. But transformation doesn't happen immediately. We have to unravel what's been knit together. As knitters know, sometimes frogging knitting isn't easy. The yarn snags and the unraveling halts so the knitter can pick apart the knot. Without this process, transformation into something else is impossible.

We can change. We can start something new. We can be transformed just like the yarn we decided to repurpose or upscale. Our raw materials have so much potential. Each of us is one of God's skeins given to the world. God is the knitter, and with God's help we are knit into our best selves.

Reflection Questions

1. Make a list of your untapped potential.
2. What is God calling you to be?
3. What do you need to unravel and repurpose?

CHAPTER THREE
THE HISTORY OF KNITTING

Uncovering the history of knitting starts with the discovery of the oldest piece of knitting in existence, a multicolored sock. For hundreds of years, people have knit socks for warmth, for protection, for fashion, and most importantly as a way to connect with others.

Starting with the American Revolutionary War and continuing through World War II, hand-knitted socks created a sense of community among knitters, as well as a caring and compassionate connection with soldiers whose survival depended on them. Thousands upon thousands of socks knit through time have carried the love and prayers of their creators to soldiers. The history of the knitted sock demonstrates how knitting can manifest love, create connection, and become a spiritual practice.

There is nothing more important than warm, dry socks. Ask any skier, hiker, or runner. They are a vital part of their equipment. A soldier, carrying a fifty-pound rucksack on his back while running through the mud, is very aware of how important socks are. Wet, cold feet can immobilize even the strongest person. Who knew that the foot has more sweat glands than any other part of the body? Keeping feet warm and dry is essential to healthy feet, and that requires the right kind of socks.

Feet are different shapes and sizes. They require a stretchy fabric that fits and forms a warm protective layer around the foot. The use of knitted fabric was more effective and comfortable than animal skins, matted animal hair, or woven fabric because of its flexibility. Knitted socks hug the feet, providing more protection and enabling the wearer to stay out in the cold longer and possibly prevent blisters, cuts, and other damage.

The oldest piece of knitted fabric, a remnant of a sock, was found in Egypt and dates from the eleventh and thirteenth centuries. The beauty and colorwork of this ancient sock suggest that knitting wasn't just about necessity. Sock knitters know that knitting tube socks is the fastest way to warm feet. Cast on, knit the desired length, and then decrease for the toe. Constructing socks that start from the toe and require turning a heel and finding the correct amount of stitches so the sock clings to the calf (a type of sock knitters call "toe up"), takes time, patience, and skill.

Knitting is definitely older than these socks. Someone had to figure out how to turn a heel, weave together the toe, and manipulate two different colors of yarn. I picture knitters trying different methods, exchanging information, peering at each other's work to see how to improve it until they found the perfect method. This sock is the culmination of innovation through time.

Communities of knitters passed down techniques and ideas just like they do today. The knitter of this old Egyptian sock created more than just a functional piece of clothing. The complexity of a pattern like this takes time and care. We knit beautiful complex patterns because they express who we are as artists. It is a way that we can give a piece of ourselves to others. This sock is evidence of the innovative and expressive nature of the craft.

Egyptian knitting spread into Spain either through the Islamic Conquest or perhaps the Crusades. By the fourteenth century, examples of hand-knitted liturgical gloves worn by bishops matching their chasubles (a poncho-like garment worn over vestments) were in use. They were knit using very small stitches out of luxury yarns such as silk. Although some gloves were made from woven material and sewn together, the knitted gloves were a better fit. They were decorated with sewn-on medallions made out of precious metal. The bishops wore the gloves when they wore their miters (hats) and removed them when they were at the altar. I picture the knitters bent over their work, laboriously creating each tiny stitch with yarn the thickness of a spider's web. We know that this extremely time-consuming process required patience and perseverance resulting in a beautiful pair of ornamental liturgical gloves. This creative and expressive act of knitting added to the pageantry of the liturgy.

It was during the fourteenth century that the "knitting Madonnas" appeared. We know that knitting did not exist during the time of Christ, but that didn't stop the medieval painters. Ambrogio Lorenzetti of Siena painted a beautiful domestic scene of the Holy Family showing Mary sitting next to Jesus on the floor, her knitting on her lap. Joseph is sitting across from Mary, and Jesus is gesturing like he is in the middle of a story. This image is a window into the imagined childhood of Jesus. Mary as the knitting mother evokes domestic tranquility as the non-anxious presence, busy creating something with her own two hands surrounded by her family. Another fourteenth-century painting by Vitale degli Equi shows Mary holding her knitting and caressing Jesus's chin with her finger. The painter has captured a tender moment between mother and son, Mary dropping her work, stopping long enough to interact with her child, her face full of love.

The discovery of the knitting Madonnas is a gift. They are the icons for knitting as a spiritual practice. Knitters know how the rhythmic clicks of the needles calm the mind and open the heart. We can see a deep love expressed on Mary's face in both of the paintings. This is the same love that we can cultivate in the spiritual practice of knitting and praying with Jesus. We visualize ourselves in the scene knitting with Mary, her son by our side watching and listening as we talk about the preoccupations of our lives. As we knit, we gradually let go of our distractions. The act of knitting connects us with Jesus, Mary, and the community of knitters through time.

Knitting as a way of connecting, especially between mothers and sons, escalated after the start of the Revolutionary War.

Colonial women gathered together at their church to spin and knit so they would not have to rely on British imports.[1] Their production of garments and knitted goods were critical to survival. For eight-and-a-half years, women knit socks and sewed garments to deliver to soldiers. They ventured out in the snow, searching for the trail of bloody footprints, and followed them even if they had to cross enemy lines. I wonder what these women were thinking as they knit their socks. Were they praying for the recipient? Were they thinking about the danger? I'm sure the blood in the snow or the sight of soldiers with rags on their feet drove the women to knit more socks, their eyes straining to see the stitches as they worked by dim candlelight through the winter months.

How many knitters and how many hours were involved in creating the three hundred pairs of socks that were delivered to the soldiers at the Valley Forge encampment? William Lee invented the knitting machine in 1589, but hand-knitted socks were stronger and lasted longer. Knitting beautiful socks (or liturgical gloves) is a creative act, while producing socks for the army is an act of patriotism, perseverance, and compassion. As a knitter who has spent many days leading up to Christmas trying to complete a pair of mittens for everyone in the family, I can imagine the drudgery of knitting sock after sock for the desperate men of the Continental Army. It was the women who labored for just over eight years to keep the army warm and protected. They knit for their loved ones, they knit for strangers, and their knitting saved lives.

After the Revolutionary War, knitting to connect with others took the form of charitable acts. Knitting was a way of responding to the gospel. Women gathered in churches to knit garments for families living in poverty. Soon they were teaching their recipients to knit.[2]

---

1. Anne MacDonald, *No Idle Hands: The Social History of American Knitting* (New York: Ballantine Books, 1990), 28.

2. Ibid., 44.

Teaching others to knit is an excellent example of living into the gospel because teaching creates relationships. Teaching empowers others in the creative act of knitting something useful like a sock or something comforting such as a blanket. The act of creating is transforming. There is such joy in watching a new knitter slowly complete each stitch and looking up triumphantly at the end of a row. I have seen people in homeless shelters learning to knit. Two heads bending over the work, the instructor encouraging them, guiding their hands, and with these compassionate gestures showing the new knitter that they are important, they are cared for, and they can create.

During the Civil War, socks took center stage once again. Women in the North and the South received word that their loved ones were suffering from frostbite and blisters. Organizers in the North called all church societies to devote themselves to the "sacred service of the country."[3] What were these knitters thinking as they knit socks to support the soldiers in this brutal war between the states? I imagine mothers praying fervently for the war to end and for their boys to come home. I see young women on both sides knitting socks for strangers' feet and knitters writing personal notes of encouragement that the men would tuck inside their uniforms. One Cleveland woman composed this short poem:

> Brave Sentry, on your lonely beat
> May these blue stockings warm your feet
> And when from wars and camps you part
> May some fair knitter warm your heart.[4]

Many of the same knitters who knit during the Civil War answered the call from the Red Cross to knit for Uncle Sam during World War I. Knitted socks could mean the difference between life and death. They stood between frostbite and trench

---

3. Ibid., 100.
4. Ibid., 105.

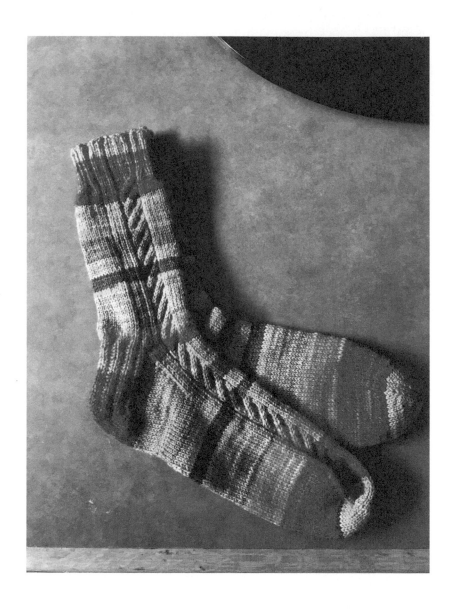

foot, conditions that killed approximately 2,000 Americans and 75,000 British soldiers in World War I.[5] The cold, wet, and muddy conditions of trench warfare caused capillaries in the foot to start to break down, resulting in dead tissue which led to gangrene. Severe cases required amputation. Soldiers needed to change their socks often in order to stay dry and warm. As a result, knitting socks as well as vests, balaclavas, hats, and mittens became a patriotic duty.

Even men and children joined women in a three-day Knitting Bee in Central Park in August of 1918. The Comforts Committee of the Navy League organized the event, which raised $4,000 and contributed fifty completed sweaters, forty-eight mufflers, forty helmets, and 224 pairs of socks. By the end of the war, knitters had made twenty-four million military garments and six and a half million garments for war refugees.[6] Women who had lost sons in the war continued knitting for the sons of others, pouring their grief into their garments. The last stanza of the poem "Knitting Women" by Kathleen Norris published in 1918 expresses it well:

We are the knitting women; weaving strong

A web of prayer; our eyes with tears are dim,

But, wife or mother, we shall search for him.

Across the seas, morning and even-song.

Lord God,—we pray—look down on what we do!

Bless this our work, help us to play our part.

The God of Battles—Father, still Thou art

The God of waiting—waiting women too![7]

Knitting during World War II continued under the auspices of the Red Cross. It was a unifying activity for the country, and

---

5. "What Is Trench Foot?" accessed November 12, 2019, *https://www.healthline.com/health/trench-foot#causes*.

6. MacDonald, *No Idle Hands*, 199.

7. Ibid., 237–38.

although machine-knitted garments could be produced, they did not carry the love and connection of something handmade. Knitters argued that hand-knitted socks and other garments were free, lasted longer, and helped those back home feel like they were participating in the war effort. Eleanor Roosevelt personified the World War II knitter by carrying her knitting with her on her travels and knitting every possible moment. Even Eleanor, who wrote extensively, had time for knitting. Her public knitting created a connection with other knitters.

Socks are still important to soldiers. During Army Ranger training, the soldiers can spend days wading through swampy water in hot and humid weather. Part of their training is learning how to take care of their feet. Each day they are given time to take off their boots and wet socks in order to air dry their skin. This mandatory rest time allows their skin to thoroughly dry, since wet feet create dangerous conditions that can result in cellulitis.

There is no longer a need for hand-knitted wool socks since soldiers can buy socks with antimicrobial and moisture-wicking properties that are especially designed for these circumstances. The nationwide sock-knitting for soldiers may be over, but knitting continues for the troops as a way of expressing love and appreciation for their sacrifices. Operation Gratitude and many other organizations like it have sent over two million care packages that include hand-knitted items to the troops overseas. Knitters know how knitted objects are an expression of love that connects us through time and space.

Knitters continue to express their feelings of love and grief through knitting. After the Tree of Life synagogue shooting in Pittsburgh, a young girl said she wanted to hug all the people who were hurting. Her mother, a knitting instructor, started the Tree of Life Project by encouraging knitters to knit the Tree of Life pattern into squares and make them into blankets for the Pittsburgh synagogue. She told her daughter that the knitted blankets would be how they could hug the families of the eleven people who had died. There was an immediate response.

Within two months, knitters had made over one thousand tree of life squares to make into blankets.

Knitting helps people find purpose in their grief, and it is a visible sign of caring. Knitters know how long it takes to knit a pair of socks or even one square for an afghan. Each piece represents a commitment to the person or to the cause.

Take Time to Reflect

Discovering Beauty: Knitting Lace

Look at the rainbow, and praise him who made it; it is exceedingly beautiful in its brightness. It encircles the sky with its glorious arc; the hands of the Most High have stretched it out.

—Ecclesiasticus 43:11–12

Who came up with the idea of lace? I can imagine the invention of knitting because people needed a method of making warm clothing besides slaughtering animals and using the skins. The first "sweaters" were probably knit to be dense and warm. Certainly, there were no holes. For people in cold climates, there is nothing better than a fisherman's knit sweater with lots of cables that add extra layers of warmth.

Lace is not for warmth, lace is for beauty. We wear something lacy because it is beautiful, light, airy, ethereal, and a wonder to behold.

I watched a woman making lace at one of the fiber festivals, deftly snatching up bobbins and twisting them, pinning the spider web thin strands into a complex pattern. It was mesmerizing. All of her efforts were being channeled into making an object of beauty. The knitter who decides to channel her energies into a piece of lace is choosing to celebrate beauty. Those of us looking on can appreciate and celebrate with her. Opening our eyes to the beauty around us is necessary for our spiritual lives. We see the actual spider web and marvel at the small creature that shaped it, or we watch the leaves changing color providing a color palette or the ice dripping off the bare branches of a tree forming a natural crystal chandelier. We see beyond what we have come to take for granted. The superficial sights point to the intricate designs underneath, and in them we see the vastness of creation.

Reflection Questions

1. How does the act of knitting help you see differently?
2. How do you balance practicality and beauty?
3. Take a close look at a piece of lace. Let your eyes see the shape, shadows, and colors. What do you notice?

Learning from the Past: Top Down or Bottom Up?

Give instruction to the wise, and they will become wiser still;
teach the righteous and they will gain in learning.

—*Proverbs 9:9*

Fifty-odd years ago, there were no circular needles, no magic loop, no interchangeable needle sets, and certainly no internet with YouTube instructional videos. Most knitters followed the same patterns. Sweaters were started with the ribbing on two straight needles. Socks were knit with four or five double-pointed needles. The idea of knitting a sweater from the top down or socks from the toe up for the majority of knitters was not yet a possibility. When these methods became popular, they were considered major innovative milestones. The idea that you could actually try on a sweater as you knit and decide if you wanted it longer or shorter based on your yarn quantity was unthinkable.

For those of us who used the same method for years, it's difficult to switch. I bought yarn and a pattern for a sweater because I loved how the sweater looked on the model. Then I realized it was knit from the collar down. Instead of decreasing toward the neck, I'm increasing from the neck to create the yoke. The pattern wants me to place stitches on holders for the sleeves. After the body is done, the stitches for the sleeves will be picked up and knit separately. I usually knit the sleeves together. Now I'm going to have to count the rows to be sure each sleeve is the same length.

Younger knitters are probably saying, "Okay, Boomer, get a grip, there are advantages to trying new methods." New methods engage the mind, which helps us to be present in the moment. During the increase row around the yoke, I have to be aware of the stitch markers and remember to increase in the stitch both before and after the marker. There is a time for mindless knitting, and there is a time for being present.

It's hard to be a beginner, especially when we are used to being an expert. Those of us who have been knitting for years have our favorite cast-on methods, bind-off methods, and construction methods. The more adventurous knitters are probably excited to try something new, but not me. I don't want to change my methods. I can vary my experience with different stitch patterns and color work. But I must change.

If we keep saying prayers we have learned by rote, they lose their impact. How many times have we uttered the Lord's Prayer? I remember when a priest changed the translation from the traditional to the contemporary version during a liturgy. The congregation was horrified. The priest offered a Lenten study and introduced different translations and musical settings of the Lord's Prayer. The study group went through the prayer line-by-line, taking it apart and discovering the richness of the words and the nuances of the translations. The Lord's Prayer was never the same. The prayer took on a deeper meaning for the congregation.

We need to encourage each other to try different methods, learn new prayers, and study the old ones.

Reflection Questions

1. Do you always knit using the same construction method?
2. What prayers or scripture do you say the same way over and over?
3. Try a different translation. How does it enhance your understanding of the prayer or scripture?

CHAPTER FOUR
OUR PERSONAL KNITTING HISTORY

My personal history of knitting and my spiritual life start with my maternal grandmother. She was a devout Roman Catholic with seven children, and I was her eldest granddaughter. I attended church with her whenever we visited. I remember snuggling next to her in the pew on Sunday, listening to the music, the drone of the congregational responses, and feeling a little put out when I was forced to stand or kneel. She didn't seem to mind. She would take my hand and escort me to the railing for communion. As we knelt at the railing, she would whisper in my ear that God loved me very much. It was in her embrace that I felt a visceral sense of God's love, and it was in her embrace that I learned to knit. I can still feel my grandmother's arms around me, her hands over my hands, slowly guiding my fingers holding the yarn and the needles to create stitch after stitch. With her hands guiding mine, I was able to knit, but as soon as I was on my own, I was overwhelmed. Manipulating two needles while keeping the yarn tight required more coordination than my eight-year-old hands could manage. But my grandmother was patient, and I was her sole focus, and who doesn't love that kind of attention? She sat with me whenever she came to visit, repeating the motions I needed to learn.

The learning continued in my third-grade class. Our teacher insisted that everyone in the class learn to knit. She wanted us to develop our small motor coordination before teaching us cursive writing. Between my lessons in third grade and the many visits from my grandmother, eventually I was able to knit on my own. My mother was always close by to pick up the stitches I dropped and to show me how to fix my mistakes. It didn't take long before I was able to pick up my own dropped stitches. I was now a creator. I had started to master my grandmother's superpower. Each time I picked up the needles, I was reminded of her love and patience. My hands were her hands. Even though she lived far away, knitting brought her close to me. It still does even though she died over thirty years ago.

I connected my grandmother's embrace at the altar rail with the love of God. This feeling was reinforced every time I sat close to her to have a knitting lesson. Her loving physical presence suggested that intentional spiritual knitting can create a connection with God.

Take Time to Reflect

For from the greatness and beauty of created things
comes a corresponding perception of their Creator.

—*Wisdom of Solomon 13:5*

I remember my first sweater. It was a cardigan with some faux pocket flaps made with chunky red yarn on size 13 needles. I think I was in fifth or sixth grade when I finished it. The buttonholes were larger than the buttons, so the sweater wouldn't stay closed, but I was very proud of it. I had successfully transformed balls of yarn into something recognizable. It was even something I could wear. This first sweater meant I had graduated into the inner circle of knitters. I could make something.

I spent my school years trying to master the art of knitting. One year for Christmas, my mother bought me yarn. She had seen me admiring a blue pullover sweater with red and white stripes. The yarn was a worsted weight, and I found it much harder to knit on the smaller size 8 needles. There was a lot of weeping and gnashing of teeth; the yarn was reknit so many times, it began to fray. A few skeins fell prey to the dog, and the sweater morphed into a striped scarf. Like many failures in life, there were lessons to be learned. The mistakes I couldn't fix forced me to find a new way to use the materials. My sock-knitting friend Georgia once told me, if you can't fix it, flaunt it. Knitting became a great teacher of life lessons and an activity that connected me to the women in my family.

When I got to college, I took an introductory class in biology and my professor was a knitter. She was absolutely fascinated with the study of life and addicted to knitting. She allowed us to knit in class, and she constantly referenced the parallels between the process of knitting and cell replication. Knitting is the same process as cells replicating in the womb, differentiating and forming the piece of the body encoded in the cell's DNA. Multiple cells join together to create different tissues, and tissues join together to create organs and we are formed. It all starts with just a few cells that begin to replicate and in time become a human being. This is the miracle of life.

This observation in my biology class and the feeling of what seemed like unconditional love from my grandmothers helped awaken a desire to become more familiar with the ultimate creator who knit me together in my mother's womb. I wondered if knitting could help me deepen my relationship with God?

Reflection Questions

1. Who taught you to knit? How old were you? What was the experience like?
2. What part of this summary of the history of knitting resonates with you?
3. What memories does the activity of knitting bring back to you?

Connecting Through Time: Making Memories

It is the smallest of all the seeds, but when it has grown it is the greatest of shrubs and becomes a tree, so that the birds of the air come and make nests in its branches.

—*Matthew 13:32*

I have my grandmother's sweater. She must have used size 2 needles because the stitches are so tiny and precise. It could be mistaken for machine knit. The sweater is a pastel orange, definitely not my color. It hangs in my closet draped over a hanger with the paper that crackles when I touch it from the dry cleaner stuffed inside. I can picture her knitting, the sweater on her lap, yarn by her side, thinking about the finished product. It's a cardigan and the buttonholes are perfect. She even put a ribbon lining underneath the button band. She cared about the construction of this garment just as she cared about her grandchildren. Her love for us felt unconditional and expressed itself in the perfect peanut butter and jelly sandwiches, with the peanut butter spread right up to the edge of the bread and the sandwich cut to our specifications—in quarters for me, diagonally for my brothers. She read us books, listened to our stories, and took us to the five and dime to buy us toys.

Touching the stitches on the Creamsicle-orange sweater brings all those memories into the present. I sometimes wonder what will happen to that sweater. After helping my mother clean out her house where she had lived for over thirty years, I realized that her treasures are not my treasures. Her memories are not my memories. We can pass stories on to the next generation, but they lose energy through time.

Just a few days before she died, my grandmother held my three-month-old son. He was the only one of my children that got to meet her. I will always remember the look of love on her face as she stared at her first great grandson. She traced a finger over his chubby cheeks remarking on his long eyelashes and perfect lips. Her eyes smiled at his eyes as they locked their gaze. He doesn't remember that moment, but I do.

Someday, whoever cleans out my things will come across the orange sweater and be surprised. They will ask each other, I never saw her wear this, did you? Maybe one of them will remember it was my grandmother's, maybe not. It's not important. Material things hold the meaning that we give them. What is important is the love we pass on to others, the memories we make with them that they can take into the future.

Some of the most beautiful memories are made in the small moments of connection. It's tugging hard on a toddler's shoe, feeling the foot slip inside, and seeing the grin on his face because it means you get to go outside to play. It's covering a child's hand with yours to help stir the last bit of flour into the chocolate chip cookie dough. Each of these countless little moments are small prayers that we offer up to God with a profound sense of thanksgiving. They connect us with each other, and they connect us with our creator. It is the accumulation of these small moments that form the loving relationships we have with each other and with God.

Reflection Questions

1. What are some of your favorite memories?
2. What family stories continued to be passed down and why?
3. What small things are you most grateful for?

CHAPTER FIVE

LEARNING THE CRAFT FOR NEW AND ADVANCED KNITTERS

Learning something new can be a humbling activity, especially when we are used to being competent. We all reach an age when we know how to navigate our world. We pass through space and time, confident of our movements. We know what to expect. Trying something new can be uncomfortable, particularly if we can't master it immediately. However, when we are contemplating a new spiritual practice, stepping outside our comfort zone is exactly what we need. Engaging childlike curiosity opens us up to new possibilities.

What happens if I wind the yarn around the needle the opposite way? What if I hold the yarn in my left hand instead of my right or vice versa? What happens if I twist stitches around each other? What happens if I drop a stitch? Few people like to feel uncomfortable. Some of us don't want to experiment. There are times when all we want is to get it right. We want to start off our knitting careers making a sweater that looks like the picture in the magazine with the six different cable patterns. We want to intuit the rows and rows of charted knitting symbols and have them magically appear on the needles with not one stitch out of place. After all, why spend hours simply knitting row after row that only produces a bumpy, uneven garter stitch?

But knitting takes practice. Musicians play scales, pitchers throw balls, and knitters make loops over and over. Every skill starts with the basics. Ballerinas spend hours at the barre practicing basic movements that form the foundation for the complex turns and jumps. Knitters learn two different ways of making stitches and realize the combinations are endless. If you can cast on, knit, purl, increase, decrease, and cast off, you can make almost anything. These simple stiches are the building blocks of knitting. They can also become the building blocks of a prayer practice.

Having a beginner's mind opens us to new possibilities. We slow down and focus on exactly what is in front of us. We have to be in the present moment. When was the last time you didn't even know how to start? Imagine, you don't know how to knit and someone lays down two knitting needles, a ball of yarn, and says, "Knit a sweater." Your beginner's mind feels helpless. When we don't know what to do or where to start, we are open to others for help. We understand that we can't do it alone.

Experienced knitters know how to knit socks in their sleep and how to create a sweater without a pattern. Knitting is second nature, and their minds can be in countless different places while their hands work the yarn and the needles. Knitting their usual way doesn't slow them down or help them to be in the moment. Fortunately, there are many challenging skills for advanced knitters: brioche, Fair Isle colorwork, lace, Aran cables, marling, and sequence knitting, to name a few. Picking a new skill slows us down and focuses our attention back on the task at hand, bringing us into the present. Contemplative prayer is about being in the present moment. Knitting can help us focus, slow down, and calm our thoughts.

If you want to learn to knit, find a knitter. I would say with confidence that ninety percent of knitters will happily show you how to knit, even if they have never taught anyone. Knitting, like any other skill, takes some time and perseverance to learn. There are many great videos on YouTube showing new knitters how to cast on and knit their first few stitches. What YouTube is missing is the presence of another human being giving you encouragement, telling you you're doing it right, or reassuring you that your weird way of holding the needles is perfectly okay.

If you want to learn to knit in order to create a spiritual practice, all you need to know is how to cast on stitches, knit, and cast off. Acquiring these skills may take some time, but learning can be part of your spiritual practice. Once you have found your knitting teacher or you have signed up for a class, collect your materials. Some classes provide yarn and needles as part of the class. If supplies aren't provided, pick out a skein of yarn that speaks to you. Make sure it's not too fine or too bulky. Fine yarn can be challenging to a new knitter, and bulky yarn can split if your aim is off. Find a yarn that feels nice in a color that you love. Check out the ball band for the suggested knitting needle size; remember that the higher numbers are the larger needles.

Teachers know that students have different learning styles. Some people are visual: show me how it's done and then I'll do it. Others want to be told what to do: this is how you hold the needles and make a loop with the yarn. And then there are some who need a guiding hand on theirs, physically doing the motions. Knowing your style and what you need will make the process less frustrating.

As you pick up the needles and yarn to begin, pay attention to what this experience is like. Be your own observer, and monitor your reactions to the learning process. How do you respond to mistakes? Are you quick to start over, quick to hand it over to the instructor to fix, or do you try to take a moment to figure it out? Don't judge your reactions, just calmly observe your preferences. Knowing yourself and your preferences will help you when you start your spiritual practice. Focus on what is happening right in front of you. How does the yarn feel in your hand? How are you able to apply tension to the yarn? How are you holding the needles?

Learning to knit can be helpful in bringing us into the present moment. When we focus on something new, it's hard to think about anything else. Our minds are fully engaged in trying to complete a sequence of small physical movements that at first feel awkward. Everything around us melts away, our world becomes our hands, the needles, and the yarn. Our eyes focus solely on our fingers manipulating the needles and the yarn. Note what it is like to have a narrow focus.

Remember learning to drive a car—your hands clutching the wheel, every sense on high alert, trying to keep the car on the road between the lines, mailboxes dangerously close to the passenger side mirror? You couldn't even take your hands off the wheel to turn on the radio. After years on the road, we travel great distances without even remembering how we got there.

It's hard to stay in the present moment once we have mastered a skill. I used to be all about the end product and not about the process. How fast can I get this knitting project done? I've knit some simple sweaters in front of the television totally unaware of my hands knitting stitch after stitch. I didn't care. I wanted the sweater just like I wanted the kind of life that comes from being grounded in prayer. But I didn't want to work at it. I didn't want to spend time in prayer. For me, just sitting still is extremely difficult.

I can sit still if I knit. Knitting brings me into the present moment. Even though I can knit and purl without thinking, I can decide to be intentional about the process. I start by thinking back to my beginner days. I remember my grandmother threading the yarn through my fingers. Here is how to hold the yarn to create tension so your stitches will be even, she told me. I feel the softness of the yarn, the smooth wood of the needles, I notice how my fingers guide the yarn around the needles, pulling just right to create the next stitch. I feel myself relax as I sink into a rhythm. If I start thinking of something other than my knitting, I stop and intentionally notice what is right in front of me. Feel the yarn, feel the needle, and start the process again.

In order to recreate a beginner's mind, advanced knitters may want to learn a different method of knitting. Try continental

Learning the Craft for New and Advanced Knitters

knitting. Learn how to "pick" the yarn instead of throwing it around the needle. Feel what it is like to be a beginner again, how awkward it feels keeping the yarn taut because you're holding it differently. Learning a different method will help slow you down and become present to the process that now feels like second nature.

Contemplative prayer needs a beginner's mind, one without expectation, a mind that is open, curious, and without censor. Prayer needs a mind focused on the task at hand instead of jumping around from one thought to another. I am making a vest that has multiple Aran cable patterns. I only work on it when I'm alone in the house. Just one interruption and I'm totally lost. It's rare that I offer my full attention to any activity. Taking on this knitting challenge puts me outside of my comfort zone and helps me focus. I have to fight not to think of other things while I try to track all the various patterns. I know if my mind wanders, I'll have to take out the row.

Learning to knit or trying more advanced knitting techniques is the first step to quieting the "noise" we experience through the barrage of stimulation and distractions that exist in our environment.

Exercises

Beginning Knitters

1. What did you notice about yourself when you first tried to knit? Did anything distract you?
2. How did you learn to knit?
3. How long did it take before you felt comfortable making stitches?
4. What happened when you made your first mistake?
5. Some new knitters end up with more or less stitches than when they started. Did this happen to you? If so, what if anything did you do about it?
6. What advice would you give a new knitter?

Advanced Knitters

1. Pick a knitting challenge that employs new skills.
2. How did you approach the project? Did you start right away? Did you review the new skills on YouTube? Did you engage a more experienced knitter to help you?
3. Were you able to master the new skill immediately, or did you have to take out your knitting and start again?
4. What was the most difficult part of learning a new skill?
5. Did this exercise require all of your attention?

Observing your thoughts as you begin the learning process, focusing on a new technique, or taking up a challenging project are all good precursors to starting a spiritual practice. The idea is to discover how to focus our attention. This will become useful when we begin our prayer practice.

Take Time to Reflect

No Worries: Learning to Let Go

And can any of you by worrying add a single hour to your span of life?

—Matthew 6:27

Learning to knit as an adult can be challenging, especially when you are anxious. Cheryl had battled anxiety most of her life. She decided to take up knitting as a way of calming herself. She signed up for a spiritual knitting retreat. At the retreat, she was paired with an older, very experienced knitter, Gloria, who seemed to have infinite patience. I watched her struggle to insert the needle into each stitch. The yarn was pulled so tight she couldn't poke the needle through, so she slid the stitch to the end of the needle to try to make it easier. The stitch dropped off before she could insert the needle, causing several additional stitches to unravel and making it difficult to fix. Cheryl hung onto the yarn like it was the rope that would save her from drowning.

Gloria knew immediately that Cheryl's anxiety had worked its way into her knitting. Cheryl needed to let go of her worries and relax. She gave Cheryl a skein of baby alpaca yarn to touch and hold and then she asked her what she was worried about. Cheryl told her that her only child had just left for college and she had spent the last few weeks worrying about him. Was he getting enough to eat, was he studying, was he safe riding his bike around campus? He had only called home once, and he was too busy to text her.

Gloria had Cheryl just sit with the yarn in her lap. She explained that anxiety was only good as a motivator to do something in the present moment that would help ensure a better future. For example, Gloria told her, if you are anxious about a test, then study now. If you are anxious about having clothes to wear, do the laundry. If you are worried about having enough money to retire, work on a savings plan. If a situation is out of our control, the only action we can take is to pray. Gloria suggested that Cheryl pray for her son, first giving thanks for him and then giving up her worries to God. She told her to just sit and feel the softness of the pale blue baby alpaca yarn in her lap. Imagine the yarn is her love for her son and she is able to touch and feel her love.

After days of sitting with the yarn and giving up her worries to God in prayer, Cheryl reconnected with Gloria. She brought back the skein of pale blue baby alpaca and asked Gloria is she could help her make it into a scarf that she could send to her son. After a few dropped stitches, Cheryl began to knit a garter stitch scarf for her son. She poured her love and prayers into each stitch. As she relaxed, she noticed that the scarf became slightly wider and her stitches became loose and easier to knit.

We all get anxious, and sometimes it can be paralyzing. The first step is to be aware of our anxiety and try to understand what is causing it. Is it something within our control? Can we do something now that will make it better in the future? If it is something out of our control, we can pray the serenity prayer and try and let it go. We only have the present moment. Worrying about the future robs us of the present moment. Knitting, feeling the yarn, and working the needles can help ground us in the present.

Reflection Questions

1. What anxiety is preventing me from living in the present?
2. What can I do today to help myself in the future?
3. What is outside of my control?

Ask for Help: Discovering the Joys of Community

But she came and knelt before him, saying, "Lord, help me."

—Matthew 15:25

I have a box that has been sitting in my closet for over two years. I opened it for the first time right after it was delivered. Then I packed it up and carefully placed it back in my closet. Every few months I get it out and open it again. The box is full of beautiful expensive yarn, the kind you want to pick up and marvel at the depth of the colors and the softness of the wool. I play this game with the box because I'm intimidated by the sweater pattern. It uses bobbins (a device that holds small quantities of yarn that makes it easier to knit with more than one color). I didn't own any bobbins, and the very word in the pattern caused me to put the yarn back in the box for the first year. I finally bought some bobbins, but I was afraid to start. I wasn't sure about the techniques in the pattern, and I didn't want to ruin this very expensive yarn.

As an experienced knitter, I help people with their knitting. But we all need help. I know at least five knitters who would gladly sit down with me and help me get started on this incredible sweater. All I have to do is ask.

One of the most popular prayers, sometimes the first prayer people say, is simply, "God, help me." This is the first step in admitting we can't do it ourselves. We need the love of God, the knowledge that there is something greater that will provide the courage to navigate the challenging times of our lives. Asking for help is an invitation to community. When we don't, we are cheating ourselves out of the chance to form a community of willing helpers that would love to offer their support and encouragement.

No matter what we are trying to do, it is easier to accomplish within a community that is focused on the same goals. This could be starting a new prayer practice or working on a challenging knitting pattern. Admitting we need help is a way of allowing others to offer themselves as a means of ministry. Sitting next to another knitter, looking on, offering advice and encouragement becomes a way of accompanying the knitter on their journey. It is helping them take the raw materials of their potential and get them working to make something that is worth making even though it may be difficult. Asking God for help frees us. It may also help us to ask others, to admit that we can't go it alone, and give us the guts to make ourselves vulnerable.

We are taught to be self-sufficient, and we tend to live in the illusion that we don't need anyone else, but we do. We need each other. Learning to ask for help with a knitting project is good practice for being able to surrender ourselves to God. Through the process we understand that we are not alone, we don't have to know everything, and we can make ourselves vulnerable with those we trust. I made an appointment with a more experienced knitter, opened the box, and started the project.

Reflection Questions

1. How often do you ask for help?
2. Do you find it difficult to ask for help? If so, why?
3. Make a list of people you trust that you could ask to help you when you need it. Say a prayer of thanksgiving for the people on the list.

Understanding Directions: Seeing the Big Picture

Let the same mind be in you that was in Christ Jesus.

—Philippians 2:5

Watching a child take their first steps is thrilling. It's the subsequent steps that are scary. The child is focused on moving forward, totally missing the step down from the kitchen to the living room or the toy on the floor that causes their ankle to roll. Parents spend weeks bent over at the waist rescuing their toddlers from certain falls. It takes practice for new walkers to adjust their footsteps to changing landscapes.

This can be true for knitting directions. Our focus is on knitting and purling the right stitches, accumulating inches, and keeping our eye on the prize of that finished garment. Armholes and neck shaping happen at the same time. Woe to the knitters who stop reading the directions too soon and only decrease for the armhole. When they joyously finish their armhole decreases and read the horrifying words "and at the same time," they realize that they should have been decreasing for the neck as well.

The frustration of making this mistake leads to finding ways to avoid it. Now, I read the directions and highlight phrases like "at the same time." I look at the picture of the finished sweater and keep it in mind while I'm knitting. Patterns with schematics are even better for the visual knitters who can see that both sides should be decreasing at the same time.

Paul reminds us in Philippians 3:14 to press on toward the goal of the prize, which is the heavenly call of God. In order to deepen our faith, we need to know where we are headed. When we understand the goal, we can take the right steps to reach it. When we first start to pray, it takes all of our energy to commit to finding a time to sit down, pick up our knitting, and open ourselves up to the love of God. Our thoughts are so focused on staying with the discipline, keeping our eyes on the road, and making the next stitch that we may forget the reason we are there in the first place. "Let the same mind be in you that was in Christ Jesus" (Philippians 2:5). Our prayer time is a chance to fully embrace the love that Jesus showed others in the gospel stories. Our goal is to embody the love of Christ in the world that desperately needs love and kindness. Prayer gives us the opportunity to reflect on how we can demonstrate that love to others.

Reflection Questions

1. What was your initial motivation for starting a spiritual practice?
2. Are you experiencing tunnel vision?
3. What would it mean to be in the same mind as Jesus?

Trying a Different Way: How to Slow Down and be Present

You must understand this, my beloved: let everyone be quick to listen, slow to speak, slow to anger.

—*James 1:19*

I attended a spiritual retreat a few years ago where we were asked to sit in prayer for about fifteen minutes and then draw a picture using our nondominant hand. The picture could be anything that came to mind. It was an interesting exercise since it let the participants be more concerned with what they were drawing rather than the quality of the drawing. The emphasis was on the process rather than the end result. Our focus can shift when we change our process.

This is true with our knitting styles. Pace is important. Frenetic knitting is not calming. We've all done it. We have sat up long into the night desperately trying to finish the baby gift in time for the shower or the last pair of mittens for Christmas. The drive to finish, produce, get it done takes over, and our focus becomes the end result.

For a long time, I knit because I wanted the particular sweater I was making or because I wanted to give someone a gift. It was all about the finished product. Then I met Debbie, a woman who was intrigued by the process of knitting. She was more interested in how different yarns behaved rather than the garments they could produce. She spent hours swatching before she even started a new project just to see what type of needle worked best with the yarn. Her pattern notes on Ravelry (see chapter twelve) would advise knitters that a certain brand of wool slides off metal needles but sticks on the bamboo.

Debbie would buy one skein of yarn from several different manufacturers to determine which yarn would best show off the pattern stitches. Her descriptions of the advantages and disadvantages of the different yarns is almost poetic. She wholeheartedly immerses herself into the project and writes notes on every pattern describing how she has modified the instructions to ensure a better fit. She has tried over a hundred different ways to cast on stitches, and she can describe why a knitter would pick one method over another. Debbie is always trying different methods and learning something new. She takes her time and invests herself in each project. This way of being has helped her to be more available to the people in her life.

Trying new methods of knitting, different ways of casting on, or a different technique can help increase our creativity by enlarging our perspective. Immersing ourselves in a project can help make us better listeners. "I'm not thinking about how I want to respond when people talk to me," Debbie explains. "I hang on their every word, giving myself over to the person and honoring their story. Being attentive to my knitting has taught me to be attentive to God and to people."

Trying a different knitting method can help us slow down, pay attention, and learn how to really focus on what's important.

Reflection Questions

1. What is it like to knit using a different method?
2. What do you observe when you slow down?
3. Invite someone to tell you a story and practice your active listening.

PART TWO

HOW TO START
A KNITTING PRAYER PRACTICE

CHAPTER SIX
THE KNITTING PRAYER PRACTICE

A prayer practice consists of praying, reflecting, and then taking the appropriate action. Every step is important. We could decide to pray, but if we don't reflect on our prayer life, what's the point? If our reflections don't result in living a life that acknowledges our dependence on God and a desire to obey the great commandment to love others, what are we doing other than sitting and enjoying the calming effect of knitting? Prayer is a practice that leads us into a life focused on discipleship. When we pray, our decisions to take action in our lives come from being open to the love of God. God's love is a powerful motivator and pushes us beyond our comfort zone to help and receive help from others. Prayer changes everything.

Beginning a Spiritual Practice

The desire to pray comes from God; the decision to pray is up to us. The idea of a spiritual practice to deepen our relationship with God sounds wonderful, but actually starting and sustaining a spiritual practice is challenging. It's important in the beginning to know what's behind our desire to deepen our relationship with God. Why start a spiritual practice now? What do I believe about God and prayer?

If you have ever tried to learn an instrument, you know that motivation to practice ebbs and flows. We've all been on diets.

It's easy at first, and as time wears on it gets harder. One of the ways to get through those inevitable challenging times in the future is to understand why we are making a commitment to practice in the first place. James Clear in his book *Atomic Habits* explains the difference between outcome-based habits and identity-based habits. Losing ten pounds is the goal of the outcome-based habit. Considering myself an athlete and eating a healthy diet because it is a great way to fuel my body for maximum energy is an identity-based habit. Identity-based habits help us continue past reaching our initial goals.

Prayer is not a goal-oriented activity. It's part of our identity as practicing Christians. Prayer is our response to God's call to be in relationship.

For a long time, I didn't have a spiritual practice. I thought it was a good idea to pray and I knew it was the way to deepen my relationship with God, but the only time I prayed was in church. I was hesitant to pray on my own, and I didn't understand why. A spiritual director helped me discover that I was afraid of what God might ask me to do. I was convinced that God would demand something from me that I wouldn't like. I thought that opening myself up to God would change my life, and I liked my life the way it was. I didn't want to feel compelled to make any changes. But in spite of those feelings, I found myself consulting a spiritual director about prayer.

The spiritual director asked me about my image of God. It was left over from my childhood. I had developed an idea of God at an early age of an old man complete with the full gray beard and wild Einstein-like hair sitting on a throne. This God was judging me, tracking my faults, and figuring out how to rain down punishments. The fact that I had a relatively good life created a cloud of anxiety. My life was too good to be true, something bad was bound to happen, and it was just a matter of time. As a young adult, this image did not coincide with what I had learned about God by studying Jesus, but still the image of the stern, crazy father lurked in my brain, preventing me from forming a deeper relationship. I didn't trust God.

No one wants to deepen a relationship with someone they don't trust. My spiritual director suggested I work on my image of God and told me to read *Your God Is Too Small* by J. B. Phillips. This wonderful book helped me understand that I was hanging on to a negative image of God. The book even had a subheading for my preferred image called "The Grand Old Man." Phillips describes how these limited ideas develop and then explains how to reconstruct an idea of God that's expansive. We need an image that is trustworthy and inviting.

Phillips goes on to say that the first step in knowing God is knowing Jesus, the expression of perfect humanity, the Jesus who said yes to the will of God. "Anyone who resolves to do the will of God will know whether the teaching is from God or whether I am speaking on my own" (John 7:17). It's only when we practice the will of God, the way of love, that we begin to understand the character of God. We know from Jesus that the will of God is for us to love God and then to love others. J.B. Phillips is adamant that it's only after we do the will of God that we will begin to know God.

> "Now the moment a man does this, even temporarily and tentatively, he finds himself in touch with something more real than he has known before. There is a sense that he is touching a deep and powerful stream that runs right through life. In other words, the moment he begins really to love, he finds himself in touch with the life of God." God is love after all and it is the opening of oneself to that love that changes everything.[1]

I was fortunate to have a spiritual director who helped me understand that I was a beloved child of God. Aligning my will with God's will could only result in the best possible path forward, and the only way to align was to be in relationship. The

---

1. J.B. Phillips, *Your God Is Too Small* (New York: Touchstone, Simon & Schuster, 1997), 83–85.

mechanism was prayer. I chose the Jesus prayer, and the repetition of that particular prayer helped me melt away my childhood image of God and replace it with an image informed by the ministry of Jesus. My repaired image of God was merciful, loving, and welcoming. As I prayed, I could hear Jesus saying, "Do not be afraid." God became the loving father of Jesus who fosters the power to love everyone.

Prayer did change my life, and the changes made a good life even better. I discovered that when life becomes challenging and things go wrong, even in the worst moments of grief, prayer makes it better. Prayer is the connection to the divine love, an endless supply of energy that sustains us through low points.

My motivation to explore my relationship with God came from having my first child. I had studied biology, and I understood the reproductive system and embryology, but it still felt like a miracle when they placed my child in my arms. How could all of these processes work together to form another human? It was so complex. The love I felt for my son went beyond anything I had ever experienced. There must be something more to this, I thought. My childhood experience with the church left me believing that there is a God and I could communicate with God through prayer. Between an excellent spiritual director, Tyler Dudley, and my priest at the time, the Rev. Lance Robbins, who preached about God's love in every sermon, I started to believe that this loving God could be part of my life in a profound way. I just needed to be willing to accept the invitation to pray. So I said yes. My belief in a God who would accompany me through life became part of my new identity as an adult. I was ready to form a prayer practice.

I began my new practice with all the intensity of a newly-wed on their honeymoon. I prayed the daily office, I prayed the Jesus prayer, and I went to every weekly eucharist that I could find. My priest raised his eyebrows when I described all the things I was doing. At the time I wasn't thinking about how I was going to sustain all of this new activity. Instead I was focused on how prayer was enriching my life in ways that I never thought possible. Opportunities to use my gifts opened up to me. Teachers that I needed appeared. Decisions were clear. I noticed that nothing seemed to happen while I was praying but my outward life was different. Then the inevitable happened. It was impossible to sustain all of my new practices while trying to work and take care of my children. The answer came to me one day as I was knitting.

Daily knitting helped me stay calm in the midst of working a stressful job and taking care of children. Perhaps I could combine knitting and praying and make my time commitment more realistic. I needed to set up a practice I could sustain.

Step one: What is my motivation? I want to know God. I want help with my life decisions. I want to proclaim the love of God with my actions.

Step two: What do I believe about myself that will help me sustain a spiritual practice? I believe that I am a beloved child of God and God will help me sustain a spiritual practice.

Step three: How do I incorporate knitting into my practice? There are many answers to this question, but I needed something specific to get me started.

I went to look at my stash, and there was a large ball of homespun yarn given to me by a friend. It was one ply and the color of pink lilacs. The thickness of the yarn varied from fine to chunky. It was obviously the product of a new spinner, and since I didn't have any specific plans for it, I decided it would be my prayer yarn. It was already special since it was a gift. I had the yarn.

I chose size 6 metal needles that had belonged to my grandmother. They were dark green, and I remember her teaching me the difference between size 6 and size 9 needles. She showed me how the number had a line underneath it so the knitter could determine the number. I thought that was genius. Size 6 needles could handle the different thicknesses of the yarn. I had the needles.

Now I needed a time and a place. Trying to figure out a time to fit this into my life every day was not going to be easy.

I am not a morning person, yet once the day starts, my time is not my own. There are countless demands coming from work, children, and just the everyday activities necessary to maintain a home. How could I stop once I jumped into the day? It had to be first thing.

I decided to knit for five minutes every morning before the kids got up. I chose a large overstuffed armchair in a quiet part of the house. I put my chosen yarn and needles on the coffee table next to the chair and set an alarm. The next morning, I got up 10 minutes earlier, did my usual morning routine, and then settled into my chair with a cup of coffee. I sipped the hot coffee and stared at the yarn and needles, giving thanks for the two women who had given me the tools for this spiritual practice I was about to start—my grandmother who loved God and my friend who was so generous with her gift of yarn.

I set my five-minute timer, picked up the needles, and cast on. I ended up with twenty-two stitches. Instead of just knitting, I found myself knitting the trinity stitch. When the timer went off, I was jolted back to reality. For five minutes I was feeling the mystery of the Trinity through my knitting. My fingers were creating three in one and one in three and a pattern was appearing. I wanted to stay in the moment, but the day was looming with all of its activities and a mountainous to do list. I carefully placed my newly created sacred knitting back in the basket, pushing the stitches away from the point so they wouldn't fall off. It would be there tomorrow waiting for me to pick up. The knitting was a reminder of God's presence. God with us inviting us to reach out and connect. For the rest of the day, when I passed by the armchair with the knitting displayed on the coffee table, I felt comforted. There lay visual evidence of my prayers, a reminder of my connection with God.

Every day, I got up and sat with my knitting. Some days I prayed for specific people, some days I just knit, my mind on nothing except the feel of my body in the chair and my fingers on the yarn and needles. The rhythmic clicking of the green metal needles like a train covering ground on a track seeming to propel me forward, even as I sat deep in the cushions, my outer world contracting to just this chair.

Think about how to set up your practice. It's like knitting a swatch—absolutely necessary but nobody likes to do it. Preparation can save us from having to start over.

We start with what we believe about ourselves and God. Some excellent starting questions: What is my image of God? Where did this image come from? The answers are never simple. My Grand Old Man image came from pictures I had seen in children's bibles. It came from watching my maternal grandfather demonstrate his powers every summer by swimming long distances under water. It came from the priests in church. It came from hearing God called father and from many other sources.

Some forty years later, my image has changed. It can vary depending on where I am and what I'm doing. If I'm on top of a mountain, my image is the scenery in front of me; if I'm holding a child, my image is the face of the child; if I'm working in the garden, the image is the lush harvest. Sometimes the image is the idea of divine arms reaching out to encircle the entire world in a cosmic hug. My images carry a sense of eternal beauty, an enormous reservoir of love spilling over and covering everything in its path like fast-moving lava full of energy, creating new land in the midst of the sea.

Preparation Exercise

1. What is my image of God?

Get a Post-it pad and a pen. Write down one image of God per Post-it note. Include past images as well as current images of God. Try to get to at least twenty different images. Keep writing even if they seem "wrong" or "silly."

Create a timeline of your life. Label major milestones with the year and short description: 1979—graduated college. Take your Post-it notes of your images of God and add them to your timeline. How has your image of God changed, or has it? What events/people/places have contributed to your images of God? Is your God too small? Is this the God you want to know? If not, do you need some help constructing a more expansive image? If so, that is the next step. If not, go to question 2.

2. What is my current motivation?

My initial motivation came after the birth of my first child over thirty years ago. I wanted to know this power of love that enables the circle of life. This was powerful motivation. Enough to help me push through my fear. Through time, motivations change and my current motivation is different. As I age, I become more aware of my finitude. I find myself wanting to know the good shepherd. I want to walk beside the good shepherd as I grow older, to feel the comfort of God's guidance and love.

3. What yarn and needles do I want to use and why?

This is an important yet individual question. We need to find the yarn and needles that are right for us, and they need to be something we care about. This is not the time to use those ugly skeins of yarn you bought when you thought self-striping meant creating beautiful stripes and not amorphous blobs. Or that leftover ball of scratchy wool from the sweater you gave to the secondhand store because it left a rash on your skin. This is the time to find a material that fits with your idea of sacred. Is there a color that fills you with joy, a sensation of softness like baby alpaca that stops you in your tracks? Does the smell of lanolin from wool bring your heart back to a sacred moment with your mother? Picking your yarn is picking your prayer partner for this endeavor. Yarn is created from living breathing animals or plants, or sometimes both. My current special yarn is a combination of 58 percent Mongolian cashmere and 42 percent linen. This unique mix of animal and plant fibers creates a translucent effect when knit with one strand and an opaque effect with two strands held together. It encompasses a good part of God's creation in an unlikely pairing that creates a soft fabric that drapes easily. It's white, it's soft, it's strong, and it's unusual. It came in a bag made of material stolen from Cinderella's tutu, tied with an ivory satin ribbon, nestled in a box overflowing with white tissue paper. This yarn screams sacred.

What needles are worthy of such a selection? I chose a wooden circular needle, size 6, made from hard birch with a gray finish. The tips are pointy enough to enter the stitch but not so pointy that they will split the yarn. Although the wood has a hard finish, it provides enough stickiness to keep the stitches from straying from the needle. The combination of cashmere and linen needed a needle made from a tree.

What is your ideal yarn? What does it represent to you? What will feel good in your hands? What will bring you pleasure in the moment? Take your time, find the right materials.

4. Where do I want to practice?

Just like Cinderella, we need our own little corner. If possible, try to find a special spot that can house your sacred knitting undisturbed. This should be a place that is relatively free of distractions. You don't want to set up in front of the laundry room or kitchen where there is a perpetual amount of laundry and dishes to be done. You actually want a "time-out chair." Find a spot in a corner, drag over a chair, and try it out. Yes, you can get rid of the cobweb or dust the baseboard and do whatever you need to do to rid the space of any obvious distractions. Just make sure the chair is fairly comfortable and you can knit in it.

Once you have decided on your location, find a place close by to store the knitting you will work on during your prayer time. If you have young children or pets that may get into your yarn, you'll need to keep it in a zippered bag. Using the same spot will help signal your brain that it's time to pray. It's like walking into the laundry area. You're there to do laundry. You don't typically hang out in that room. Your prayer corner has a purpose.

5. When do I want to practice?

The only time that works for me is first thing in the morning. I've tried every other time of day, and it just doesn't happen consistently. Something always gets in the way. I can be assured of interruptions, distractions, and even a lack of motivation as the day wears on. However, if you are awakened by an infant in the morning or you are struggling to get kids out of bed and to school, maybe mornings aren't the best. Maybe it is your lunch hour, maybe it's your child's quiet time, or maybe it is right before you go to bed, your work is done, and the house is quiet. What's important is to find a similar time each day so the practice becomes a habit, like brushing your teeth after you get up in the morning, and if you happen to skip it, something feels off. The practice needs to become as important as getting dressed. Putting it into your routine will help keep it consistent.

6. When will I start?

Choose a time when you will be home in your regular routine. Don't pick the week before your vacation or a major holiday. Write the time you have picked on your calendar every day for a least the first month. Before you start, observe what is going on around the time that you have set aside for your prayer practice. What possible distractions or obstacles might cause a problem? Can you take any action that might mitigate these possible problems? As you approach your start date, think about what might make your practice more enjoyable. Did you pick the right yarn and needles? Do you have your spot ready? Is it comfortable?

7. What will I make?

This is not about making anything, it's about praying. However, knitting does produce fabric that can be made into something useful. It's fine to just knit a swatch like I did when I used my friend's yarn and the trinity stitch. You could decide to knit a prayer shawl or a sweater or just about anything. Whatever you decide, it should not be something that requires all your attention. The Aran sweater with twelve different patterns on the back and stitch markers every six stitches is not what you want to use for prayer, but the hours of stockinette stitch required for the back of your husband's sweater is perfect. The circular lace shawl with spiderweb-like yarn fits the special yarn and needle category but doesn't work as a prayer partner unless it's the fifth time you've knit this pattern. Keep it simple.

Beginners

Start with the garter stitch. Cast on any amount of stitches and knit. Turn and knit another row. At the end of your prayer time, stop and count your stitches. Did you drop or add any? If you dropped stitches, it's time to learn to increase. If you added stitches, knit two together. Don't worry about trying to pick up a dropped stitch or how you might have inadvertently increased a stitch, just knit during your prayer time and observe how your fabric grows. The mistakes aren't important. Mistakes are how we learn. The fabric that begins to form is a metaphor for our lives. There are holes, occasional excess, and things we have dropped, but as long as we make corrections, we can get back on the path.

Experienced knitters

Pick something to knit that doesn't require all of your attention. I picked a sweater knit in the round from the bottom up. It is just knitting round and round using a single strand of yarn for six rows and then a double strand of yarn for six rows that creates a stripe effect. It takes three minutes per row, so instead of using a timer, I simply knit two rows. It should be something that will let you relax while your knit, something that keeps you in the present moment because the yarn and needles feel good in your hands, but still lets your mind focus on the presence of God. You know what that means for you.

The actual practice

At your appointed time, sit in your chair with your yarn and needles on your lap. Take a deep breath and relax your body. Notice how it feels to be sitting in your chair. Feel the yarn and needles. Ask God to help you stay in the present moment and to be aware of God's loving presence. Begin to knit. If a stray thought comes into your mind, let it go. Maybe you remember something you need at the grocery store. Have a piece of paper and pen nearby to write it down and let it go. If you think of a sick friend, offer a quick prayer to God for healing and then let it go. If you wonder whether you should quit your job, tell yourself you'll think about that later and let the thought go. We can't control the thoughts that come into our heads. We do have control over whether or not we decide to entertain them. The Russian Orthodox talk about thoughts that invade our prayer time as birds that land on a tree branch. We don't need to let them build a nest, we can shoo them away. Others describe the thoughts as sticks floating by on a river. We watch them as they come close and then we let them drift away. We are just observers.

If you are like most people, it may not feel like anything is really happening during prayer time. We can remind ourselves to be aware of the presence of God and to invite that loving presence into our hearts to heal and transform us, inspiring us to share this love with others. Using a method of reflection like the *Examen* helps us become aware over time of how prayer makes a difference in our lives as we continue our practices. We ask ourselves questions about our lives and where we see God at work. We connect our spiritual lives to what is happening around us.

In 2017, there was catastrophic flooding in Houston, Texas. People posted on social media that they were praying for all those affected by the flood. Cindy—the rector of my church—and I were praying for the flood victims when we decided our prayer practice was calling us to action. But what could we do? We were in a small congregation located in one of the most impoverished areas of Rochester, New York. We continued praying. Every day, I sat with my knitting wondering how we could show the love of God to the people of Houston.

We decided to find a church like ours in Houston and ask them what they needed. I got on the internet and searched for small congregations. I stumbled on Lord of the Streets, an Episcopal mission that focuses on relationship-based ministry with the homeless. I called, and Steve, the vicar, answered the phone. He told us what was most needed. We put out the word to the congregation and set up a table in the front of the sanctuary to place our offerings. Every day, I prayed for the people of Houston, especially the homeless. Love and concern for them wove itself into the knitted fabric that grew in my lap. Soon, we had a mountain of jeans, packages of underwear, new socks, and bags of travel-sized shampoo and soap. We would say a prayer of blessing over the offerings at the Sunday service on Labor Day weekend and then ship everything to Houston.

Two women we had not seen before joined us for worship that Sunday. They looked like a mother and daughter. When Cindy began to talk about Lord of the Streets, she was interrupted by the younger woman. She raised her hand and was waving it saying, "Oh, oh!" Cindy called on her and the young woman blurted, "We're from Houston and we volunteer at Lord of the Streets!" We sat stunned. How could this happen?

After the service, we found out that they were in fact mother and daughter. They had gotten one of the first flights out of Houston to come to upstate New York to look at colleges. When I asked them how they decided which church to attend, the daughter told me she googled churches in the city of Rochester. They attended St. Mark's in Houston and volunteered at St. John's. Our church is St. Mark's and St. John's, so they decided to attend our service. They were thrilled that a small congregation over fifteen hundred miles away had taken action to help the homeless in Houston. All of it was the result of praying and talking and figuring out that we need to be in relationship with one another. Prayer opens us up to relationships. It helps us take the right action.

Now you're ready to start. You know your motivation, you have your materials, your place and your time. As you begin, reflect on what's working and what's not working. Try different places and times until you find what works for you. Teach your family that your prayer time is sacred. Be aware of potential obstacles you might encounter that will prevent your practice. Track your progress like you track the rows of a pattern. Give yourself a mark or turn a counter every time you sit and pray.

Take Time to Reflect

Stitch Markers: Marking Your Journey

The Church Year consists of two cycles of feasts and holy days: one is dependent upon the movable date of the Sunday of the Resurrection or Easter Day; the other, upon the fixed date of December 25, the Feast of our Lord's Nativity or Christmas Day.

—*Book of Common Prayer, p. 15*

There are many different types of stitch markers available. They range from plastic colored circles to sterling silver charms. A simple search on Etsy reveals the creative ways crafters make it beautiful and fun to mark a pattern on the needles. A stitch marker means stop, something is going to happen with the next few stitches that will require your attention. For most knitters, they are absolutely essential for complex patterns and helpful for simple things like marking the start of a row on circular needles.

My favorite projects are full of cables. I use colored markers to remind me that the Celtic knot I am knitting is done on the stitches between the red markers, the honeycomb stitches between the two purple markers, and so on. Sometimes markers are used to designate where an armhole begins or shoulder shaping. Markers can be very helpful in defining a pattern.

Dates of the liturgical year are markers for the spiritual life. They help define spiritual patterns that provide context throughout the year. I grew up in this context, but I didn't discover how important it was to me until I went adrift. When my last child graduated from college, I realized that I had been living in the context of the school year. When September came and went without any shopping for school supplies or the need to attend teacher conferences, I experienced a sense of loss. These events had been the stitch markers for my life.

This is when I rediscovered the liturgical year. I began to pay attention at church. The color of the vestments went from green to blue, the season from Pentecost to Advent. The new church year was about to start. It was a perfect time to make the seasons of the church year become the markers to help me create a new way of ordering my life, a new pattern for deepening my spirituality.

Advent, the season of waiting, was a wonderful way to begin. I knit through the four weeks focused on a beautiful blue baby blanket to honor the liturgical color for the season and to remember the birth of Jesus. It was the first year our family didn't put up a Christmas tree until Christmas Eve. We intentionally celebrated the entire twelve days of Christmas and welcomed Epiphany with a bonfire out in the snow. I knit a white shawl during Epiphany, complete with sparkling crystal beads to celebrate the season of light. I committed to forty inches in forty days for Lent and created my first Lenten cowl using a deep purple yarn. The fifty days of Easter became a time to create hats out of beautiful luxurious scrap yarn for women who were completing their chemo treatments. The hats were a celebration of resurrection. Then in ordinary time, I was back to knitting cute little animals for baby gifts, market bags, beach cover ups, and airy shawls for summer nights.

Each season has a purpose and is marked by special observances, colors, prayers, and music. The liturgical carousel spirals through time, bringing us along for the ride deeper into its patterns, each cycle providing new insights. It's a different way of marking time. The focus is not on the passage of time, but rather on how we live into time beyond just being stuck in the linear motion. The purpose of the seasons is to remember milestones in the story of the church and to rekindle our awareness of these *kairos* moments so we can delve deeper into what it means to be Christian.

Reflection Questions

1. What is your favorite liturgical season?
2. How do you celebrate the liturgical seasons?
3. What knitting projects will help you mark the seasons?

The Lost Yarn: Learning to Live in the Present

Devote yourselves to prayer, keeping alert in it with thanksgiving.

—*Colossians 4:2*

I can't find my blue mohair yarn, and I have searched the entire house. Twice. It all started when I read one of my favorite knitting newsletters that typically highlights one or two patterns. This time I noticed a lovely but simple crew neck sweater on the front page. I glanced at the yarn requirements and discovered the sweater was made holding three strands of lace weight yarn together, two mohair and one smooth. I filed the information somewhere in my crowded brain and continued on with my day.

About two weeks later, I took a friend on a yarn crawl. She had recently moved to the area, and when I discovered that she was a knitter, I knew I had to introduce her to all of our local yarn stores. One store had the most beautiful royal blue mohair yarn on display next to a deep blue lace weight yarn that would be perfect for the simple crew neck sweater I had just seen. I wanted it immediately, but then I reminded myself that I had two mohair yarn projects on the needles that were hibernating because I don't like working with lace weight mohair yarn. I actually have to look at the needles when I knit with this yarn. The yarn is sticky, and I have to use needles with extra sharp points just to poke the tips into the loop. Plus, I had decided that

I was not going to buy any yarn on this expedition. I told myself I needed to finish at least one project before buying anything else. I talked myself off the ledge and left the store empty-handed.

The yarn haunted me. It took over my thoughts until I went and bought it. I started the sweater immediately. The three strands were a perfect combination, and with size 10 needles the back of the sweater grew at an amazing rate. Soon I was working on the armholes. To keep my project bag small, I only carried the three working balls. When the yarn ran out, I went to look for the extra balls but I couldn't find them anywhere. I had planned on finishing this sweater on our vacation. Turning the house upside down the night before a vacation is not a good practice. I tried to convince myself that the yarn would turn up.

I was angry during the search. I wondered why. Losing things makes me feel out of control, stupid, in addition to the disappointment of not getting what I wanted. Here I was, ready to go on a spectacular vacation, angry over some lost yarn even though I have a roomful of yarn and projects. Material things can take on a lot of energy and keep us from really understanding what our feelings are trying to tell us. This entire project had taken over my mindshare from the very second I lusted after the royal blue mohair yarn. I allowed it to take over my thoughts, and it kept me from living in the present moment.

The present moment is where God is, and it's where our life is. I know that I often live inside my head either in the future or the past. I allow in thoughts that take over and distract me, so I don't remember where I put my keys or my phone or my yarn. Learning to live in the present takes a high level of awareness. Praying can help create this awareness.

A few weeks later, I went rummaging in my linen closet for a particular set of sheets. My hand landed on what felt like a bag of yarn. I pulled it out. There were the additional skeins. I had thrown the bag into the linen closet to protect the yarn from the dog. Sometimes letting go is the best way to get something back.

Reflection Questions

1. What was the last item you lost?
2. How do you bring yourself back to the present moment when your mind wanders?
3. What do you need to let go?

Resistance: Working Through Our Fear

Surely God is my salvation; I will trust, and will not be afraid, for the Lord God is my strength and my might; he has become my salvation.

—*Isaiah 12:2*

Some days, I spend my free moments thinking about knitting. I imagine what project I will work on when I finally collapse on the couch, and I can almost feel the softness of the yarn in my fingers. I am amazed at the level of pleasure I experience by just thinking about my knitting practice. Then I get home and I'm too tired to knit. I try and guilt myself into it. *You need to pray, you've made a commitment to a practice, it's only four rows, it only takes ten minutes, if you can't do it then how do you expect other people to do it, and on and on. . . .* In the time I have spent arguing with myself, I could have done the practice. What is my problem?

My resistance is high, and I'm channeling the rebellious teenager who stomps off to her room and slams the door yelling, "I'm not going to do it." What is that about? There is a part of me that is selfish and lazy, that just wants to shut down, turn off, and watch mindless television. She wants to eat whatever she wants, quit going to the gym, quit praying, and quit having to deal with the challenges of life. A glass of wine and the new season of the latest Netflix show is far more appealing than digging out the spiritual knitting project.

But it's more than just feeling tired or lazy, it is true resistance to the practice. It's about fear.

Fear can cause resistance. When we start a spiritual practice and open ourselves up to God, we need to trust God. Like any relationship, we have to spend time getting to know each other. With God, this happens through scripture, worship, and prayer. Maybe we are starting to experience a calling, or a nudge to make some changes in our lives. Maybe we are discerning a call to focus on our health, spend some time volunteering, forgive the person who made us miserable, or whatever has come up as we sit with God. Prayer can bring up a holy host of ideas that may complicate our lives.

One of the commands Jesus says repeatedly is, "Do not be afraid." We can trust God. The nudges, the inspirations, the ideas that come from an active prayer life will take us to places of wonder and gratitude. The best way to conquer feelings of resistance to our prayer life is by asking the question, "What am I afraid of?" Take the fear out and face it. Pray for strength to take away the power it has over you. Pray for the strength to send it away. Resist the siren's call to ignore your practice and pray anyway. Remember you are praying to the God of love who is always there granting you the strength to overcome.

Reflection Questions

1. When have you encountered resistance to your spiritual practice?
2. What do you fear?
3. How do you draw strength from God?

CHAPTER SEVEN
THE SPIRITUALITY OF REPETITION

Practice is about repetition. It is repeating something over and over until it exists within us almost with a life of its own. The basketball player practices hundreds of free throws. When the opportunity for a free throw presents itself, the basketball player is ready. All she needs to do is allow the muscle memory to propel the ball into the basket. It is the same for the piano player who practices scales for hours. When he encounters a scale of sixteenth notes in the key of B minor, his fingers go to the correct keys. The body has been trained.

The mind can be trained as well. We use repetition to memorize multiplication tables, conjugate irregular Spanish verbs, and remember the names of bones and muscles. Repetition creates neural pathways, deepening pathways in the brain where neurons fire faster and faster because they are traveling the same road over and over.

I scheduled a private confession with an old priest. After I confessed my sins, I waited for the word of counsel. The old priest paused a moment and then recited three verses from a psalm that perfectly fit my situation. It felt like a magic trick. When I asked him how he had picked out those particular verses, he replied that the verses just seemed to materialize inside his head. This kept happening every time I saw him for confession. Each time he would recite different but perfect psalm verses. *How do you make psalm verses come into your head that fit a situation,* I wondered?

It turns out, the answer is simple, you pray the psalter. Every day and more than once a day, you sit down and pray with the psalms. The Daily Office prescribes the order, and if you choose the monthly cycle, you read every psalm once per month. Years and years of reading the psalms carved the words into the old priest's brain just like the Colorado River carved its way through the Grand Canyon. That priest not only hears my confession, he hears the right psalm verses that offer direction and comfort. It's like children clamoring to read the same book every night before bed. Soon they are "reading" the book. The repetition of the words becomes a story that is transferred off the page into their minds and then out of their mouths. Now, they can tell the story almost word for word using the pictures on the page as prompts.

Repetition is a powerful tool.

Repetition in knitting creates fabric. Loop after loop creates stitch after stitch, and soon the individual stitches form the whole. Repetitious prayer creates a fabric of wholeness by calming the mind to create space for healing. Over and over we call out reminding ourselves of the Divine Presence that is always with us. One of the most powerful repetitious prayers is the "Jesus Prayer." Repeating the Jesus Prayer day after day and year after year has profound effects.

The story of the Jesus Prayer is told in a short little book entitled, *The Way of the Pilgrim*. Nothing is known about the author or exactly when the book was written. Scholars think it dates back to the 1850s. The book starts with a person who hears a Bible verse read in worship: "Pray without ceasing" (1 Thessalonians 5:17). The scripture captures his attention, and he begins a pilgrimage to figure out how a person could possibly accomplish this task and keep themselves clothed and fed. Eventually, he happens upon a monk who tells him to be thankful that God has given him the desire to want to find out how to pray without ceasing. Then the monk teaches him the Jesus Prayer, "Lord Jesus Christ have mercy on me." The pilgrim is told to repeat the prayer three thousand times a day, then six thousand, and finally twelve thousand times a day. After days of concentrated effort, the pilgrim finds that the prayer is repeating itself in his head as he goes about his daily business. The rest of the book tells the story of how the Jesus Prayer changes the pilgrim and affects all the people he meets on his journey.

The Jesus Prayer should come with a warning. There will be healing and transformation if you pray this prayer. Repetition acts as a change agent, but only when we are intentional about how we practice repetition. Repetitive motion can either cause tendonitis or stronger muscles. The pianist who practices scales using haphazard finger positions will not be able to manage sight reading difficult music as well as the person who employs the proper fingering. We want to lay down the best possible neural pathways. Using repetition correctly requires intention and focus, especially when beginning a practice.

Complex knitting patterns use repetition. I knitted a fisherman-style sweater that had a twenty-four-row pattern repeat. The center of the pattern had six interwoven strands that crisscrossed back and forth, flanked on both sides by a two-stitch twist next to a six-stitch cable. Additional cables and twists branched outward from the center. For knitters who like to make cabled Aran sweaters, you know that after a few repetitions of the pattern rows, you can begin to "read" the knitting. You may memorize some of the pattern, but you are also able to "see" what to do with the cable. It becomes obvious that every fourth row requires the knitter to cable two stitches in front. It becomes more obvious when the knitter forgets to cable on the fourth row. You can see the mistake in the pattern. The pattern provides the road map that helps us create the fabric we want.

Following a pattern goes beyond the simple repetitive act of knitting one stitch after another. Following a pattern requires attention and intention. Attention is putting ourselves in the present moment. Intention is how we put ourselves in the present moment. When we first start knitting a complex pattern, it takes most of our attention. The rest of the world falls away. Even if we are listening to a podcast or watching TV, we miss a section when we get engrossed in something new. It's not until we come to the end of a row and our attention is freed up that we even realize we haven't heard a thing in the last few minutes.

Attending to new and complex patterns is a way to bring our attention to the present. We are focused on creating the right movements to make the correct stitches that form the pattern. We feel the needles in our hands, the texture of the yarn through our fingers, and if we are working with wool, we smell the lanolin. Our attention is heightened, and our mind is free from thoughts of the past or thoughts of the future. The next step is to combine this heightened awareness with intention. Perhaps we are motivated to knit a sweater for a person we love. Not only do we want a sweater without visible mistakes, we want one made with intentional love knit into the stitches.

Thomas Keating, a Catholic monk and priest, describes this practice as the "attention/intention practice." He explains that being in the present moment (focusing our attention), with the intention that all we are doing in that moment is for the love of God, is a practical way of working toward a deeper level of contemplation. He suggests that we institute a particular time each day when we intentionally do some particular work for the love of God.[1]

Knitting or any meditative repetitive activity such as crocheting or quilting is a way to start the attention/intention practice necessary for contemplative prayer. This is the very opposite of knitting mindlessly in front of the TV. The goal is to establish a practice of paying attention with the intention of using the time to focus on the love of God. We are knitting for the love of God. On a more practical level, we are knitting a prayer shawl for the love of God, or a hat for the homeless, or a sweater for my spouse, as long as the intention is focused on the love of God. Keating tells us that what we do for the love of God connects us to the divine presence. When we submit our will to God, we allow the divine energy, the love of

---

1. Thomas Keating, "The Practice of Attention/Intention," in *Centering Prayer in Daily Life and Ministry*, ed. Gustave Reininger (New York: Continuum, 2006), 17.

God, to be manifested in us, and this will become apparent in how we move through the world. Having a sense of the divine love within us changes our perspective and our priorities which motivates us to continue the practice.

When we repeat this sequence of attention and intention, we begin to establish a habit that enables us to be fully present not only in the moment but to others. To be completely present to someone is one of the most difficult of all practices. Think of the young child following the parent around as they try to do their chores demanding attention. The child tries everything he knows, beginning with whining, then crying, or getting into something, or asking a million questions. It is hard to be fully present to a young child and keep them clean, clothed, and fed. But we could probably do better. It's challenging to be present to the elderly, the sulky adolescent, the grumpy spouse, or the harassed clerk at the store. We need a practice of attention and intention that helps us begin to align our minds with the mind of Christ. The practice develops the patience to be present and allows the divine love to be expressed through us.

I visited an Orthodox monastery in Wisconsin a few years ago. The monks practiced the Jesus Prayer, and you could read it on their lips as they mowed the lawn and washed the dishes. In every moment they dedicated their work to the glory of God. They purposely repeated the Jesus Prayer over and over as they went about their chores. One of the monks told me that the repetitious prayer made his work holy and pulled him back into the present moment. There were no mindless activities, everything was important. I told him it sounded exhausting. He told me it made him feel like he was living his life fully alive.

All the monks were knitters. Instead of using a prayer rope that helped monks track how many prayers they said, the abbot required the novice monks to learn how to knit. The abbot wanted to "see" how many prayers they were saying. One monk was knitting a blanket that had a 220 stitch count per row. Each stitch was equal to one Jesus Prayer. Every night he would knit for a few hours, and the abbot would multiply the rows times the number of stitches to see how many prayers were said. The young monk had undergone a major transformation, according to the abbot. He came to the monastery with a troubled past and nowhere to go. His life before had been filled with violence and drugs, and as a former gang member his body was covered with gang tattoos that even covered his face. The tattoos were the only sign left of his past. Now there was a calm young man, head bent over his knitting, lips forming the prayer while his hands created the new fabric of his life.

What happens with repetitious prayer? The abbot told me that repetitious prayer works at opening the heart to divine love. It's like dripping water on a rock: eventually the water will wear a hole right through it, cracking it open. Initially, the young monk had a difficult time repeating the Jesus Prayer. His mind would wander and obsess over his past life. He would be distracted by feelings of anger and betrayal. The young monk baulked at learning how to knit, but once he started, he was excited to see the progress of his prayers. He had stitch markers on the sides of his emerging blanket. I asked him what they were for, and he explained they marked spiritual milestones. "This is where I let go of my anger for a particular person, and this is where I felt like I could forgive another person," he told me. There were more markers on the side as the blanket got longer. More evidence of a heart cracking open and being filled with love.

The feeling of divine love that invades the heart is palpable. Think back to the time when someone put a newborn baby in your arms, or when you greeted a loved one at the airport, or when a child wanted to climb up in your lap and give you a hug. These feelings of love come from a heart that has been opened, filled, and now spills out to permeate our lives. Our perspective changes. We begin to see expressions of the divine love in the world, and everything seems new and different.

The world changed for the knitting monk. He could see his progress. When he finished his blanket, he covered himself with his own prayers. He left the stitch markers in, and he would touch them every night and pray for the people who had hurt him and the people he had hurt. After years of knitting and praying, he told me that he wakes up with the Jesus Prayer in his head. "It is like the beating of my heart," he said. "It pumps the divine love through every part of my body, making me fully alive and open to the world in a new and profound way."

As knitters, we have an affinity for repetition. We know repetition can be calming as well as productive. We know that following a repeating pattern can produce amazing fabric that can be fashioned into a breathtaking work of art. Repetitive prayer is calming and transforming. Knitting while praying creates a visual representation of our prayers. It is a record of our practice, and the created fabric shows our progress. The basketball player measures her practice by the improved accuracy of her free throws, the piano player by the speed and accuracy of his playing, and those with a spiritual practice measure their practice by the love that begins to build up in their hearts that soon bursts out into the world.

Take Time to Reflect

Spiritual Transformation: The Bathrobe Project

Because you have made us for Yourself, and our hearts are restless till they find their rest in Thee.

—*Augustine, Confessions, 1.1.1*

Imagine a full-length long-sleeve bathrobe with a train. I have endured a lot of teasing about this project. I tell people the train is for sweeping up dog hair around the house. Right now, it's hibernating. I confess I don't work on it much because it feels so overwhelming. The large stash of yarn required for this garment assaults me every time I look in the closet. It takes up an enormous amount of space. Every time I take out the robe, I have to spend time familiarizing myself with the pattern. Once I restart, I get excited and I work a bunch of rows, and then I find myself beginning to feel overwhelmed and back it goes into the largest knitting bag I own.

The process of knitting a huge bag of yarn into a bathrobe that will cover me from head to toe has become a metaphor for spiritual transformation. I'm drastically changing the form of the yarn.

Transformation is something we regularly experience. When we are hungry, we eat and transform our condition. If we move from the suburbs to the city, we transform our circumstances. But the transformation we long for is the transformation of being—a change of heart that propels us to serve the community, a community dedicated to serving God.

This transformation is the only thing that can fill the hole in our heart. We may avoid committing to this level of transformation for any number of reasons. We don't want to face our demons, we are prone to distractions, or we mistakenly think we can fill the hole in our heart with something else—food, exercise, a closet full of yarn. But the nagging feeling persists, and it's only when we give ourselves over to God that the hole starts to fill.

The creation of the bathrobe happens through countless repetitive knitting just as spiritual transformation happens prayer by prayer, liturgy upon liturgy; like drops of water on a stone, the canyon is created and filled with life. Spiritual transformation takes time, effort, the support of a community. We can't leave it in the bag, we have to keep it visible, work on it every day, because we know our hearts are restless until we rest in God.

Reflection Questions

1. Where do you feel overwhelmed?
2. As you continue your spiritual practice, what observations have you made about changes in your life?
3. What is being transformed?

The Repetition of the Liturgy: Joining Threads Together

You have fed us with spiritual food in the Sacrament of his Body and Blood. Send us now into the world in peace.

—*Book of Common Prayer, p. 365*

I hate to weave in ends. It's taken me years to figure out how to sew together pieces of a sweater so it looks professionally seamed. I have spent hours working on seams, taking them out and trying again. Then, after all that work, I have to start weaving in the ends of yarn that are left over from changing colors or adding a new skein until I discovered, quite by accident, the magic knot. I wonder why no one has told me about this clever method of joining two yarns together? It does mean there is a small knot in the work, but I have bought skeins that have imperfections larger than the end result of the magic knot. There is one caveat, the knot has to be done right. It it's done incorrectly, it will pull apart.

There is a specific order used to tie the two ends together to make the knot. Without order, things can fall apart. What is the best way to create order? Order is created through structure. When we establish a routine, we can keep our priorities. Day-to-day life is better. But when we leave a lot of ends hanging, we know we will have a mess to clean up.

Life gets in the way of our routines. The phone rings as we are attempting to leave the house, and we leave our laptop sitting on the counter as we rush out the door with the phone to our ear. We say yes to a project that we don't want to do, and now we don't have time for our own priorities. We don't take the time to think things through, to understand the consequences of our reactive decisions, and we are left with the loose ends of projects not finished, miles not walked, and children not heard.

The magic knot is proof that there are ways to join the threads of our lives together, carefully paying attention to the order so the knot will stay tied.

This is why I love the repetition of the liturgy. There is a reason for the order. We sing praises, we hear the word of God, the gospel is proclaimed, we reaffirm our faith, we confess, we are forgiven, and then we offer one another the sign of peace. Once we have offered the peace, we offer ourselves to God, we bless, break, and bestow the bread and wine in remembrance of the one who lived, died, and rose again. Every week I may be at the end of my rope, or in this case the end of my skein of yarn, but I come together with my community and experience the magic knot of being joined together. I am fed by this ritual in mind, body, and spirit, and it gives me the strength to continue the sacred work of life.

I have come to view the thickness of the knot that comes from tying two pieces of yarn together as the strength that comes from being joined to a community through the weekly ritual of the Eucharist. It is difficult and time consuming to weave in the loose ends of our lives by ourselves. We don't have to be alone hiding our loose ends on the inside. We can come together each week and be healed and joined with others as we rediscover the love of God through the breaking of the bread.

Reflection Questions

1. How do you order your life?
2. What are your loose ends?
3. What part does the Eucharist play in your spiritual life?

Overuse: The Need for Boundaries

And on the seventh day God finished the work that he had done, and he rested on the seventh day from all the work that he had done.

—*Genesis 2:2*

If you love to knit, eventually your hands may feel sore. We've all heard of carpel tunnel syndrome and probably know at least one person who has had surgery to fix it. Whenever we do anything repetitive, there is a point where the repetition can be damaging to our nerves and muscles. When is enough, enough? We are familiar with the advice "everything in moderation," but we don't necessarily heed it. Whoever suggested moderation did not have a huge family expecting hand-knitted garments for Christmas or for their birthday or for their newborns. We are only too happy to comply since it gives us an excuse to go buy more yarn, try different patterns, and indulge our knitting passion.

But passions can become addictions.

We know we are addicted to knitting when we ignore the pain we experience in our hands, shoulders, or arms and keep knitting. It's amazing how the biological processes work against each other. Pain in our bodies is a signal that something is wrong, yet we ignore pain and instead focus on the rewards we get from knitting. Repeated exposure to the pleasures of knitting can create a pathology of the brain that overrides the pain we experience if we knit compulsively. It is easy to fall into this trap. Knitting is so different from overeating, drinking, or gambling. It is much easier to justify staying up until the wee hours of the morning to finish a gift than staying out all night at a bar.

Pain is the signal we have gone too far and it's time to take a rest. Pain should never be ignored, because like pleasure it is one of the ways our body has to communicate to us. When did we stop paying attention to our body?

If we adopt a sabbath way of life, we can mitigate the pain that comes from overuse. Regular rest is part of a healthy, holy life.

Balancing prayer, work, recreation, and rest is the way to live a healthy life. Our recreation is not rest. Sabbath is rest. Sabbath is worship. When we rest, we can spend time with God, reflect, and reacquaint ourselves with our priorities. We can retreat from the frenetic pace of the world. We do not have to over-function, over-produce, or over anything. We live a balanced life when we establish the appropriate boundaries.

Reflection Questions

1. What pain are you experiencing?
2. What is it telling you?
3. How can you implement a sabbath time in your life?

CHAPTER EIGHT
SUSTAINING A PRACTICE

We have followed the steps in the previous chapter. We have a place to sit down and pray, we have an appointed time, and we have the yarn, needles, and pattern. At first, we have been faithful to our practice. After all, five minutes a day isn't much. Sometimes we have prayed for longer, but we have done at least the five minutes. After a few days or maybe even weeks, we begin to feel ourselves being called away. There is a sense of urgency about something we need to get done instead of praying, or we are bored with this new routine or maybe we are feeling overwhelmed. Eventually we decide not to pray. This will happen, and we need to be prepared. We need to have a plan to restart.

It's easy to start a new practice; it's hard to sustain it. I think of it as a roller-coaster ride. There are times when the practice is easy, we are flying down the hill, feeling exhilarated, knowing we are on the right track. We are fully aware of the benefits of deepening our relationship with God, seeing the difference it is making in our lives, and committed to continuing. Then, life gets in the way. Our routine changes, a loved one gets sick or we do, it's crunch time at work, or maybe we just get bored. We stop taking time to pray, and we tell ourselves that we'll get back to it after vacation or when the company leaves or when we feel better or when work calms down. We are off track and stuck at the bottom of the hill. This will happen. It is only a matter of time. As we begin a new practice, we have to make sure we have a mechanism in place to deal with the inevitability of getting stuck.

One way to sustain a prayer practice is to find a prayer partner. Having another person who agrees to be your prayer partner gives you options for accountability and encouragement. Sometimes it's just about accountability. You can make arrangements to report to your prayer partner on a regular basis about your practice. It could be as simple as a text once a week that says, "I practiced five out of seven days this week" and your partner would give you a thumbs up. If you text you have practiced zero out of seven, your partner could call and together you could figure out what happened and how you might be reinvigorated. Or you could arrange with your prayer partner that if you really get off track, they will say, "It's time to call your clergyperson or spiritual director."

Sometimes it's about sharing your experiences. You might decide to get together with your prayer partner once a month and talk about your practice. You could work together on any problems you might be having. There is no substitute for another committed caring person to keep us accountable.

In addition to recruiting a prayer partner, it is helpful to be aware of our preferences and tendencies about sustaining a practice. If you play the piano or take karate or study another language, you know it is the consistent practice over time that enables progress. Sometimes our preferences can get in the way of a consistent practice. We may prefer a variety of activities, and committing to one specific activity on a daily basis is challenging for us. Maybe we take on too much, and instead of practicing five minutes a day, we start with an hour and end up feeling overwhelmed.

Understanding what can get in the way of our success in building a daily practice can help us determine what tools can help us when we get stuck. Our knitting preferences tell us a lot about ourselves. Do we prefer to start a knitting project or finish one? Are we easily bored? How do we deal with setbacks and mistakes?

What Kind of Knitter Am I?

Start by spending a few minutes analyzing your knitting practice. Ask yourself the following questions:

1. What's my yarn stash like? Do I have more yarn than I could use?
2. How many projects do I have on the needles?
3. How many projects am I actively working on?
4. How long have some of these projects sat languishing in the closet? Why do I neglect specific projects?
5. What motivates me to restart a project?

Read the descriptions below. Which kind of knitter best describes your knitting preferences? Are you a combination?

Yarn Collector

The yarn collector is the knitter who is enamored with accumulating yarn. This knitter knows all the local yarn stores and has a yarn store locator on her phone. You call her when you know you will be vacationing out of state for advice on what shops are worth visiting and she will tell you what yarns they carry. She attends sheep and wool festivals and seeks out unusual fibers. She will buy six balls of white angora on speculation and then later envision knitting the perfect shrug. Each yarn collector will have their own storage methodology. Some will carefully pack the yarn in bins to protect it from moths, cats, puppies, and children. Others will create beautiful display shelves.

One of my favorite yarn collectors has shelves on two walls of her spare bedroom full of yarn. She graciously let her knitting friends see her collection, and we all enjoyed perusing the various colorful fibers and hearing about where she had found them. Each set of skeins carries a memory from her travels.

Collectors are about the hunt. They enjoy the initial thrill of finding the most gorgeous yarn and procuring it. They spend time fantasizing about its potential. Joy comes from possessing the potential.

Our spiritual lives are full of potential. We are like yarn sitting on the shelf waiting to be transformed into a spectacular knitted piece. As a collector, the hardest part about starting a prayer practice is starting in the first place. With a huge stash, it may be hard to decide where to start. The choices are overwhelming.

If you are a collector, think about why you like collecting. Is it the hunt for a specific item? Is it the idea of having a luxurious yarn ready to be transformed? How do you feel about your collection? Sometimes, having a collection can be overwhelming. Too many choices can create a paralysis. Perhaps you picked the perfect yarn from your stash to start your practice. You have made some progress but your stash is calling you. There are other projects you have in mind, more places to go to see and buy more yarn, and it just seems futile to devote time every day to this spiritual knitting. Five minutes a day is not enough time to see progress on the sweater you have decided to knit. You are overwhelmed. You feel the weight of all the things on your to do list. Something has to go. You stop knitting and praying.

Restarting is hard for anyone. We need to be prepared with something that we find motivating. A possible strategy could be to buy a beautiful calendar and a sheet of stickers for your prayer space. Every time you sit down to pray, place a sticker on your calendar. Collectors don't like to see holes in their collections. It may seem childish or simple, but it can work. Work with another collector type of knitter. Just text each other a picture of your calendar once a month, or if you want to be more engaged with one another, meet for coffee. Share your calendar full of stickers, show off the progress you made on your knitting, and talk about your spiritual life. What are you discovering about God? What are you learning about yourself? We need to help each other through encouragement and sharing what may inspire us.

Project du Jour Knitter

This knitter is sparked by knitting samples or pictures in knitting magazines and books. "I must have that floor-length bathrobe with a train," she thinks, looking at the picture of the woman posing on the staircase in her knitted robe. This knitter walks into a store and spots a bomber jacket on a mannequin, and two seconds later she is working with the sales staff to determine if there is enough yarn for her to make it in her favorite color. She does not stop to consider if she will like how the pattern works or if the yarn pills or even if the sweater is the right design for her body type. She sees and she buys.

I know a project du jour knitter who saw a beautiful Icelandic cardigan with silver buttons displayed at a yarn store. The staff had assembled a kit that included the yarn and the pattern and packaged it in a clear cellophane bag. Here was a no-brainer purchase. When the knitter got the package home and opened the bag, she discovered there were no silver buttons in the bag and the pattern was knit in the round, which made steeking necessary. The yarn was placed carefully back in the bag and is awaiting the moment when the knitter confronts her fear of steeking. Project knitters tend to get excited initially about projects and then lose interest as the reality of knitting twelve different types of cables every other row sinks in.

The project knitter starts out with loads of energy and full of enthusiasm. As time goes on and the work becomes tedious or difficult, the project knitter loses interest. They are looking for the next fun thing, their attention deviates from the sweater that was on the cover of the latest *Vogue Knitting* magazine to the newest pattern featured on the Modern Daily Knitting website. Focusing on one thing is next to impossible. They tend to have a smaller stash than the collector, but a larger collection of unfinished objects (UFOs). If you are a project du jour knitter, then you need several projects ready for your prayer time knitting. Allow yourself to go where the energy is. Embrace your UFOs, and get them ready. Take an inventory of your UFOs.

Getting back on track is about tapping back into our initial energy. Try to remember how it felt when we cast on the first stitch and then use that energy. Organize your projects so they are ready for your prayer time. Take a picture of each project, print the pictures, and use them like a deck of cards. As you sit down to pray, pick a card and knit on that project. Reshuffle the deck for the next time.

Process Knitter

Process knitters are the most prolific. They are the knitters that sit in long meetings knitting on complex sweaters or socks without a pattern in sight. Garments magically appear from their needles. They never end up gift wrapping one mitten with an enclosed note promising the second mitten. Their knitted gift includes a sweater, hat, and gloves knit on size 2 needles tailor-made to fit perfectly.

I sat on a board of directors with Jerry who is the epitome of a process knitter. He and I would knit at every board meeting, but somehow he was finishing multi-colored, cabled, man-sized sweaters while I was working my way through a row. At one meeting, I complimented the executive director of the organization on the red and black sweater he was wearing. It was, of course, a Jerry original. Jerry knits every moment he can, loving every movement of his fingers feeling the yarn and the satisfaction of watching a spectacular garment gradually appear.

Process knitters carry their knitting with them in case they have to wait. They don't waste a moment. This group is the most prone to repetitive stress injuries. Most process knitters learn how to vary their knitting techniques so they can prevent the inflammation that comes with overuse.

Process knitters typically will not have a problem sustaining the practice of knitting and praying. The potential pitfalls for process knitters are injuries and burnout. This knitter will keep knitting even though they might be experiencing some symptoms of repetitive motion injury. If you are experiencing pain while you knit, stop knitting and consult a physician. If you find yourself resistant to this advice, it's a good idea to ask yourself why. Why are you denying what your body is telling you? Instead of knitting, spend your five minutes of prayer practice putting lotion on your hands and massaging your forearms.

Look up some exercises and stretches for your hands and do that. Ask yourself what is driving you to knit even if it hurts.

If you are a process knitter and suddenly you just don't want to knit ever again, you may be experiencing burnout. You may be spending too much time knitting and neglecting other aspects of your life. Instead of knitting, shorten your prayer time to one minute and just stand in front of a timer being aware of the presence of God. Ask for healing. Do this until you feel the slightest spark of energy, like a small plane practicing a short field takeoff. Instead of taxiing down the runway gathering speed, the pilot revs the engine while keeping his foot on the brake. When the rpms are high, the pilot takes his foot off the brake and the plane shoots down the runway like it was just released from a sling shot. Wait for your rpms to come back up before you restart your knitting prayer practice.

The Dabbler

The dabbler is the knitter who likes the idea of knitting but finds the actual act of knitting difficult. This knitter is either new to knitting or never fully developed the techniques that make knitting enjoyable. They don't really know how to fix their mistakes, so when they hit a snag in their knitting, they typically ball it up and put it in the back of the closet. They may get motivated to try again when a friend has a new baby and they think a baby blanket can't be that hard to knit until they get home with a bag full of fine baby yarn and size 3 needles. The self-proclaimed "easy" chevron baby blanket pattern made with two colors of yarn turns into an uneven striped mess with holes, and the leftover yarn gets donated to the Linus Project. Dabblers can become full-fledged knitters if they find a knitting mentor. They need someone to guide them to the right project and then help them from start to finish.

Some people just like to dabble. Go ahead and dabble. Dabblers are not completely engaged and that's okay. It's better to dabble and experience a short-term prayer practice than never experience it at all. The best option for dabblers is to identify new and different ways of praying. When the knitting part of the prayer practice gets difficult or boring, switch to using a prayer rope or rosary beads. Try praying with icons or coloring scripture quotations. Know you like to dabble, embrace it, and offer yourself a variety of different ways to engage with prayer.

Monogamous Knitter

This is a small group but they do exist. This knitter buys the exact amount of yarn required for their project and they knit until completion. Once they finish a project, they may not knit for a while until something inspires them. Usually, another type of knitter will drag them to a yarn store and parade luxurious fibers past them until they find something that tempts them to start their next project. Beware, if this knitter is in process on something, dragging them to a yarn store hoping they will buy more yarn is futile. The monogamous knitter does not have any extra yarn stashed in their house.

If you are a monogamous knitter, you are already committed to starting, working, and completing a project. The pitfall for you is that this project of prayer is never complete. You may feel yourself start to drift away when you finish whatever knitting you have decided to use during your prayer time. Typically, once you finish a project, you like to bask in the afterglow of a job well done and you are not eager to start anything right away because it means you have to commit to it until it is done. So don't start another knitting project right away. You can sit in prayer without knitting. As long as you feel committed to practicing prayer on a regular basis, you will probably keep going. If you feel forced to choose a new knitting project immediately, this could be detrimental to your prayer practice. Simply continue praying for five minutes a day with your hands laying open in your lap. When you feel the urge to knit again and the perfect project presents itself, start knitting during your prayer time. Just keep praying, and remember, your prayer project isn't meant to be completed.

Finish Avoider

This knitter has many UFOs lying around, hidden in their house. There are different reasons for UFOs: boredom, difficulty, not having enough yarn to finish the project, worried the garment won't fit, dread of having to weave in countless ends, intimidation about a technique used in the pattern. Sometimes, the reason to avoid finishing a project can happen in an instant.

One knitter was holding up the back of a very complex Aran fisherman's knit sweater to her husband's armpit to see if she should begin the decrease for the armhole. She thought it was the right length and was reveling in her progress when her husband innocently commented that he wanted the sweater to be a bit longer. The perfectly knit cabled sweater with popcorn, honeycomb, and diamond stitches sat for fifteen years in a basket near the fireplace until a puppy yanked the waiting hanks of yarn from the basket and ran through the house, tearing the yarn apart with her razor sharp teeth. Miraculously the back of the sweater was found in the basket undisturbed on the needles. The knitter turned the piece into a pillow, which sits on a shelf to prevent the latest puppy from destroying it.

Check out your UFOs. Ask: Why did I stop knitting? Is it too difficult, too boring? Is it because I don't know where I left off? Pick a project and commit to the next step. Don't worry about finishing it, just knit the next row. Considering the entire project can be overwhelming. People ask, "How long does it take to knit a sweater?" I have no idea how long it takes me to knit a sweater since I work on many different projects simultaneously.

Once, I made the mistake of timing how long it took to knit one row on a sweater coat. When I realized the number of hours it would take to finish the coat, I stopped knitting and put it away. I was overwhelmed. It took a long time for me to reinvigorate my interest in that coat. I kept seeing the pattern in my mind's eye, picturing myself in the dead of winter wrapped in the soft yarn. I dug it out of the back of my closet, and I took that sweater coat everywhere I went. I knit in the class I was auditing, I knit waiting for the water to boil for my oatmeal in the morning, I knit in the car while my husband drove us to the grocery store.

The sweater coat grew. It doubled as an afghan on my lap during the winter. It became a part of me like a good long book, and when I finally finished it, I felt like I had lost an appendage. The knitting bag that had accompanied me for over a year now sits empty near the door, but the sweater is my constant companion on cold winter days. I wrap it around me and pull it closed, reveling in the cabled borders. When people ask me how long it took to knit, I just look them straight in the eye and tell them, "Years."

Is there an unfinished project that you keep thinking about? Do you need help getting it started again? Take it to an instructional session at your local yarn store, recruit an experienced knitter friend to help, or see if there is a Knitting Guild Association meeting in your area. Just figure out the next step.

Setbacks

I picked the Shakerag top designed by Amy Christoffers in the *Modern Daily Knitting Field Guide No. 6* to use in my prayer time. I was struck by the pattern that uses a single strand of Sylph yarn from Jade Sapphire for six rows to create a transparent effect and then two strands for six rows to create an alternate opaque stripe. This luxury yarn is expensive, so I decided to substitute another yarn. I bought some beautiful hand-dyed yarn that cost almost as much as the Slyph. I had knit quite a few rows before I decided it was the wrong yarn for the project. A single strand of the yarn wasn't transparent, and doubling the yarn changed the gauge. Using this substitute yarn derailed my prayer time project. Here was the first setback.

I bought the Slyph yarn and started again. This sweater is knit in the round, and for experienced knitters, we are all aware of the line in the directions that states, "Join, being careful not to twist stitches." I carefully ran my fingers across the 220 stitches before I joined the two ends to create a circle and started knitting. I was sure the stitches were not twisted. After twelve rows, I had the sinking feeling that something wasn't right. I ran my fingers back over the knitted fabric, and sure enough it was twisted. I was knitting a Möbius strip.

I was angry that I had made such a fundamental mistake, a mistake I had thought I had taken pains to avoid. How did this happen? My prayer practice came to a grinding halt. Ripping apart my sweater wasn't going to be easy since it involved two skeins of yarn that would need to be wound back up. Now my prayer time was associated with a mistake I could barely believe I had made. I had to put the project in a bag while I confronted the fact that even experienced knitters can make simple mistakes. It took a few days before I was ready to sit down and continue my practice.

At least in knitting, we can have a "do-over." This is not always true in life. Mistakes aren't easily ripped out and reknit. As I sat there painstakingly ripping out each stitch, then stopping to rewind the yarn, I thought about the various "mistakes" I had made throughout my life and prayed for healing and forgiveness. There is no rewind button in life. We have to move forward in a different way. We have to check the stitches multiple times to make sure they aren't twisted before we join them together. We can be careful not to allow ourselves to be distracted or in a hurry.

Setbacks will occur. We will make mistakes. We can be intentional about how to deal with our setbacks. The questions we can ask ourselves are: What can I learn from this? What bad pattern can I break? What do I need to do differently?

Sustaining the Practice

Gather as much support as you can to sustain your practice before you start. If you respond well to encouragement from other people, tell everyone you know that you are starting a daily prayer practice using your knitting as a way to pray. Ask them to pray for you and to encourage you by asking you about your progress. Be prepared for setbacks. Pick a new start date and start again. We can tolerate and recover from short interruptions, but we need to have strategies in place to restart. For the piano player, it could be the upcoming lesson that creates the sense of urgency and causes them to sit down to practice after a few days off. For us, it could be the knitting partner who calls to make sure we are taking up the needles and finding time to pray. Part of our practice is learning how to restart. Sustaining doesn't mean never quitting, it means being able to start again and again and again.

Take Time to Reflect

Healing Relationships: Integrating Our Mistakes

I have seen a limit to all perfection,
but your commandment is exceedingly broad.

—*Psalm 119:96*

Sometimes a picture of a sweater pattern can take my breath away. One showed a beautiful woman with long black hair posing in a field, hair wafting around her face, enjoying the spring breeze in a celery green cotton sweater. Cables ran up and down the sweater, fanning out over her hips, back in at the waist, and then expanding again at the chest. Purl stitches filled in between the cables, generating a textured fabric, highlighting the cable. The loose three-quarter-length bell sleeves completed the romantic look. I bought the yarn, cast on, and started knitting. Then my father had a heart attack.

It was the middle of the night when my mother called. I jumped out of bed and started packing for the seven-hour ride to the hospital. I was throwing clothes into a duffle bag when my eye caught sight of the green cotton sweater sitting on the couch. I grabbed it, stuffed it into a bag, and tossed it in the car. It turned out to be my saving grace those many hours in the hospital. I sat next to my father's hospital bed, cable needle resting behind my ear, knitting my way up the back of the sweater. I made remarkable progress on the sweater, and my father made remarkable progress recovering from his surgery. After days of sitting and knitting, the back was almost done, my dad left the hospital, and I was back in the car traveling home.

It wasn't until months later that I discovered an anomaly. I was admiring the cables while pressing the garment in order to measure its length when I saw it. There, square in the middle of the back piece, was a cable missing a twist. It was the only cable on that row that hadn't been twisted. I looked harder, thinking this cannot be true, I must have made it up. I looked again, but it was still there. My eyes went immediately to the mistake. I asked some of my non-knitting friends how they liked the sweater and if they could see the mistake in the back. They couldn't see a mistake. My knitting friends would zero in on the cable and say something like wow, what an interesting pattern. Others said, that mistake is pretty far back, are you going to take it out? Now I had to decide if I was going to take out the eight or so inches of work.

Knitting is one of the rare activities where we can tear out our mistakes and redo it. It may sound appealing to be able to correct a mistake, but we pay for the privilege by ripping out hours of work.

I decided to keep the mistake in the sweater. A friend of mine told me, if you can't fix it, flaunt it. I made the mistake because I was distracted. I was probably talking to my father while I knit the stitches instead of cabling. I knew every time I wore that sweater, I would think of the time I had with my father in the hospital and how I paid more attention to him than to my knitting. The mistake became an indication of my love for my father. If I unraveled it, it would be like unraveling history.

We don't have the ability to unravel our latest mistake in life. At best, we can apologize, make amends, and try harder. We live with our mistakes, and we can learn from them. We wear them much like the sweater: they are part of us, and they can be powerful motivators for change if we are willing to examine them.

When have you made mistakes in your knitting, and how do they serve as a metaphor for what was going on in your life? Are you a perfectionist? How do mistakes help us grow?

We become who we are through our mistakes. My knitting mistake reminds me that relationships are more important than perfection. I have embraced that cable with the missing twist, and I wear it with pride.

Reflection Questions

1. Where have you made mistakes in your knitting, and how do they serve as a metaphor for what was going on in your life?
2. How do mistakes help us grow?
3. What mistakes do you carry with you?

Counting Stitches and Dealing with Distractions

Whoever holds her fast inherits glory, and the Lord blesses the place she enters.

—*Ecclesiasticus 4:13*

I hate counting stitches, especially right after I cast them onto the needles. I have to be in a quiet room where there are no interruptions. Sometimes even that doesn't work, because my own thoughts can be interruptions. I'm counting, and then I start thinking about something I need to do and I get distracted. Recently, I counted the stitches on a new project, and I was missing two. I counted them again and again and again. I find it fascinating that my solution to this problem was to just count the stitches again hoping that I was wrong the other three times. Have you ever done this? I finally had to admit I was missing two stitches.

Life is full of distractions. I grew up in a time where multi-tasking was an expected way of being, especially for working women. Trying to do too many things at once dilutes our attention, and the inevitable results are mistakes or a half-done task.

Today we can choose from a menu of distractions. Remember when TV shows were on once a week? There might be a cliff hanger at the end of the show, but we knew we would have to wait an entire week to know what happened. Today, we can jump right into the next episode and soon it's midnight and we have to force ourselves to go to bed. Or, we can pick up a cell phone no matter where we are and be connected to a world of pictures and information that provide a window into what all of our friends and relatives are doing. As part of our spiritual discipline we can decide to fast from our distractions. Pick one distraction, then designate a start and end date and go! Observe how giving up a potential distraction affects your life.

As I limit the distractions in my life, I find my ability to focus increases. Things get done, and done well.

Reflection Questions

1. What's the distraction that pulls you away from your priorities?
2. How does this distraction dilute your attention?
3. Try a time-limited fast from this distraction and observe what changes in your life.

Dealing with Setbacks

She came up behind him and touched the fringe of his clothes, and immediately her hemorrhage stopped.

—Luke 8:44

How is your spiritual practice going? Are you knitting an inch a day on a cowl or a blanket or a special project? Are you making time to spend with God? If you're like me, you may have skipped a few days and gotten discouraged. Or maybe you have experienced a setback that caused you to become discouraged. When we fall out of our practice or feel discouraged, we need to be ready with a plan to start over. We need to know how to deal with setbacks.

Imagine a four-month-old puppy suddenly picking up your entire knitting project in her needle-sharp puppy teeth and shaking it like it's an animal she just caught. Imagine trying to stay calm while chasing the puppy who is leaving a trail of handspun yarn wrapped around chair legs and tables. The puppy is loving this new dangerous game of "I've got the best new chew toy in the world and no one is going to take it away from me."

After retrieving the knitting, I assessed the damages. It was a mess. I had to untangle the yarn and take out the project stitch by stitch. The handspun yarn seemed to be intact, but as I looked closer I saw some frayed yarn. I've knit long enough to know these frayed pieces will create an area of vulnerability that will eventually cause a hole in the garment. Once there is a hole in the knitted fabric, it will continue to grow unless something is done and the best thing to do is to unravel it and start again.

A mangled knitting project is nothing in the grand scheme of life compared to other setbacks we experience along the way. Life events such as divorce, job loss, the death of a loved one, betrayal, failed relationships, and other setbacks can derail us from pursuing who God is calling us to be. We make mistakes, we get hurt, we suffer loss, and these moments can fray the fabric of our lives. They create holes that become larger if they are not addressed. It's important to stop and unravel what has happened to us and why it has happened, and then we can figure out how to heal and restart. It's our prayer that connects us to healing. Prayer is the act of opening ourselves up to the healing love of God, and that love is what heals the frayed yarn of our experience. With God's help, we can repair the fabric.

Reflection Questions

1. What are the frayed areas in our life?
2. What needs to be unraveled and reknit?
3. What is our plan to deal with inevitable setbacks?

The Sweater Request

Therefore, since we are surrounded by so great a cloud of witnesses, let us also lay aside every weight and the sin that clings so closely, and let us run with perseverance the race that is set before us.

—Hebrews 12:1

I often knit in public, and rarely does anyone ask me what I'm knitting. People just accept the activity, especially when I'm sitting somewhere waiting. Every week I take one of our grandsons to karate. His six-year-old sister enjoys going as well, and she plays with her dolls in the waiting area while I knit. Several weeks into this routine, she stood in front of me, put both hands on my knees, and watched me knit. "Grandma, what are you knitting?" The question caused a heavenly choir of angels to start singing in my head. She was interested in my knitting. I had already taught a granddaughter how to knit, and she completed some stitches on an afghan I was knitting for her baby sister.

"I'm knitting a sweater." She was dumbfounded. "You can knit a sweater?" I could see her processing this thought while she stared at my fingers and felt the soft fabric growing from the needles. Her face brightened. "Could you make me a sweater?" "Sure," I said. "What color?" "Pink!" I told her I would take her to the yarn store and she could pick out the yarn. It took a few weeks to arrange a time. Meanwhile, I searched the internet for the perfect pattern. I found a plain pullover sweater with contrasting lace on the hem and the cuffs of the sleeves. Perfect. My granddaughter loved the lace embellishments and immediately christened the sweater her "new princess sweater."

At the store, we looked at various options of the required weight of yarn for the body of the sweater. There was only one option for the lace. The store owner remarked that this lace weight yarn wasn't as stiff as the yarn called for in the pattern but it would be the same gauge. I heard what she said, but I was immersed in the experience of delighting a grandchild with my knitting knowledge and expertise. We bought bright pink yarn for the body and a florescent purple for the lace embellishments.

We wound the yarn at the store, my granddaughter carefully cranking the ball winder, mesmerized by the transformation of the skein into what she described as a cake of purple cotton candy. The entire experience was like a wonderful dream, something I had imagined for years finally coming true. We left the store, my granddaughter clutching the bag of yarn to her chest.

A few days later, I was cursing that purple yarn. To meet the gauge, I had to go down to a size 2 needle. Even though I tried to loosely cast on, the stitches were so tight that I struggled to get the point of the needle through each stitch. I wanted to quit. Time after time I restarted until finally I put the yarn in a bag. My granddaughter kept asking me about her sweater.

Spiritual practices can turn into purple lace weight yarn. The daily effort can become challenging, requiring more effort than what we feel we can give. We want to quit but once we're in, it keeps calling us back, like those big blue eyes of my granddaughter asking how it's going with her sweater. It occurred to me that the shop owner had known what I had yet to discover. The purple lace weight I had chosen was too fine for the project. I choose another purple yarn and this time it all came together. I used two different sweater patterns and finished the pink and purple princess sweater. Watching my granddaughter twirling around rejoicing in the sweater was worth every moment of frustration. All I needed to do was figure out a different way to achieve the same goal.

Trying the same thing over and over when it doesn't seem to work leads to frustration. Sometimes all we need is to change something simple in order to get back on track.

Reflection Questions

1. What's not working in your practice?
2. What small change can you make?
3. Who might help?

PART THREE

EXPANDING YOUR PRACTICE

CHAPTER NINE
KNITTING THROUGH ADVENT

The worst time to start a new prayer practice is during one of the busiest times of the year. December is when people are frantically decorating, baking, buying presents, and trying to live into the images they see posted on social media. And yet the best time to start a new prayer practice is when our focus has been diverted from the meaning of the liturgical season. Advent is the start of a new church year, a time of waiting and anticipation. The season is lost on the person who is consumed by the demands of the culture that is focused on Christmas alone. Advent calls us to turn back to God, to remember the birth of Jesus, and to ponder the second coming. It is a time to stop and reflect on the past, the present, and the future. This can't happen if our entire month's schedule is full trying to meet unrealistic expectations. To experience Advent, we have to make room in our lives to intentionally turn back to God.

A baby blanket is a great project to knit during the month of Advent. In anticipation of the birth of Jesus, we prepare a gift, a blanket knit with love in every stitch even when we don't have a particular baby in mind.

It is best to knit a blanket with a chunky yarn so it can be completed during the season of Advent and Christmas. There are some extremely soft yarns available that knit up quickly, along with plenty of patterns in your local yarn store or on the internet. The texture of this yarn is reminiscent of the softness of a newborn's skin. This reminder of new life can be especially healing when grief is present.

As we knit, we ponder in our hearts, like Mary, the birth of Jesus. What does this mean for us? How do we follow Jesus today? Regardless of whether our faith is weak or strong, we pray for the love that came down at Christmas to be reborn in our own hearts. We give ourselves to the present moment, working in the quiet darkness of the season as we create a new, soft fabric for an unknown child. And in the midst of the present moment, we allow ourselves to contemplate the final coming. What do we think about this much anticipated moment that felt imminent in the first century? Are we prepared? What does preparation look like? These are the real questions of the season. What are these questions pushing us to do? How do we want to be?

We sit with these questions, and we knit. We knit through Advent, through the twelve days of Christmas, we knit right up to Epiphany, and then like the Magi we set out with our gift. There are always newborn babies to be found. I look for them in the NICU (neonatal intensive care unit). This is a challenging place to be during the Christmas season. The babies in the NICU float between this world and the next, their fragile, not-quite-ready bodies trying to cope with the harsh reality of life outside of the womb. I contact the chaplain and offer up the newly knit baby blanket full of Advent prayers for the new church year. Sometimes I present the blanket myself, sometimes I give it to the chaplain. It is enough to know that this gesture will let the family know of the love in the world for their child. When I have put the blanket in their hands, they can't believe a stranger took the time to make them a gift.

Knitting through Advent is a gift we give ourselves. It can re-center our attention to the real meaning of the season. The themes of Advent, hope, peace, joy, and love can center our prayer time. Each Sunday we listen to the lectionary, reflect on the scripture, and pray for the world. This is where we start with our knitting. What is our hope for our community this year? Where can we help establish peace? What joys are we thankful for? Love is this blanket we created for a family that so deeply needs to know that they are not alone.

Take Time to Reflect

Baby Knitting

Thus says God, the Lord, who created the heavens and stretched them out, who spread out the earth and what comes from it, who gives breath to the people upon it and spirit to those who walk in it.

—Isaiah 42:5

I peered into the nursery window to watch the nurses tend their tiny charges. My daughter-in-law was in the process of having a C-section, and the family was expectantly waiting. A door opened in the back of the nursery. A nurse appeared, pushing a portable crib, followed by my son still in his yellow sterile gown. The nurse positioned the crib next to the others and then bent down and picked up the baby. She handed the pink swaddled bundle to my son. His eyes widened and overflowed with tears much in the same way they had when he opened the gift from his wife on their wedding day. Here was the ultimate gift, a beautiful, healthy baby girl full of life. His miracle, our miracle, the culmination of millions of cells knit together to form this tiny body with the miniature fingers, blue-gray eyes, and rosy lips.

The process of reproduction is fascinating. Cells divide and divide and divide and then specialize just like stitches formed over and over becoming part of the sleeve or neck or ribbing. The creator knits us together in our mothers' wombs, making us each a unique individual.

I think about cell reproduction when I knit for newborns. I marvel at the teeny tiny sweaters knit with lace yarn on size 2 needles that have miniature collars and ruffled sleeves. Small details that surround the tiny fingers, flailing arms, and the absent neck of an infant. Creating teeny garments to give to pregnant women is a hope-filled task. Each stitch anticipates the miracle of life that is slowly developing and hidden safely away in the darkness of the womb. We knit with anticipation and purpose.

Advent is a perfect time to knit for an infant and reflect on the birth of Jesus, to think about God knitting love into each and every cell of his being just as we knit love into each stitch of the blanket. We build up love this way. The love accumulates along with the stitches and then when the moment is upon us, when the nurse places that child in our arms, we are overwhelmed by the depth of our feelings.

When we knit, we are the creators. When we pray, we connect with the Creator and we open ourselves to the love that changes everything, especially us. It helps us to see potential in everything, even in the most challenging situations. We pray for God's kingdom to come, and our prayer gives us the energy to help make it happen. We nurture the infant, teach the child, support the adult, and celebrate the elderly. We work with God in love to create the best possible world.

Reflection Questions

1. Why do you create?
2. Other than knitting, what else do you create?
3. Has a regular prayer practice changed your view of creation?

The Alphabet

He has filled them with skill to do every kind of work done by an artisan or by a designer or by an embroiderer in blue, purple, and crimson yarns, and in fine linen, or by a weaver—by any sort of artisan or skilled designer.

—*Exodus 35:35*

I turned on the radio and happened upon a fascinating interview with Claire Garland, author of *Knit the Alphabet*. Somehow, she had engineered a way of knitting three-dimensional letters. Her explanation about how she was able to manipulate her yarn and needles to form the perfect "S" was riveting. Each letter was a separate story of the struggles of her design process. I couldn't imagine how she had figured out the secrets of knitting twenty-six letters, but I knew immediately I wanted to make them.

I ordered the book and chose yarns that were the same colors as a classic pack of eight crayons. There were enough small skeins of bright orange, yellow, red, purple, blue, green, brown, and black washable acrylic yarn to knit up the entire alphabet. In my head, I was already in production. I pictured teaching the grandchildren phonics holding up each perfectly knitted letter. Years down the road we would laugh at how they learned to read with the knitted alphabet. This is my happy place as a knitter, envisioning the completed project, the joy it will bring, and how I get to be the purveyor of that joy.

I collected all the yarn, notions, and needles and started with the letter A. I finished the first leg and then I got stuck. Now I understood why the designer had to work so hard to fashion the letters. The project went on the back burner, stuck in a bag that hung on the back of the door of my sewing room. Every time I closed that door, it hung there accusingly, letting me know of my lack of fortitude and perseverance. The grandchildren were getting past the stage where they would need alphabet letters. I started thinking about repurposing the yarn for something else. Figuring out the directions would require too much time, effort, and energy, and for some reason I wasn't willing to sit down and work on it.

Another pregnancy was announced. The knitted alphabet resurfaced in my brain. "You have time," the voice said. "You have a few years to get this done." The bag stayed behind the door until the puppy grabbed it right in front of me, ripped it off the door handle, and took off. Crayon-colored yarn spilled into the hallway and down the stairs. I captured the dog, and as I put the yarn back in the bag, I wondered where my initial enthusiasm had gone. I sat with the bag on my lap and opened the book to where I had left off and read the directions for the next part of the letter A. In that moment, I had an epiphany: I felt stupid. I could not understand the next step and I didn't like feeling incompetent. It was uncomfortable.

The only way to improve at anything is to open ourselves up to being uncomfortable, to face the fact that we may not get it right the first time and to be willing to try it over and over until we figure out what we don't know.

I pictured the new child forming in my daughter-in-law's womb. Her chubby fingers feeling the knitted letters, her eyes bright, the giggle as she announces the name of the letter. I have three to four years to knit those letters. Help is available.

Sometimes the way to get unstuck is to think about others. I was willing to become uncomfortable in order to provide a gift for the newest grandchild. When I get stuck in my prayer life, I think of all those people who need prayers. I start there. Let me just pray for one person today who is really suffering. Sometimes all it takes is one small prayer to break us free.

Reflection Questions

1. What puts you outside your comfort zone?
2. What motivates you to work outside of your comfort zone?
3. How does praying for others help restart your prayer practice?

CHAPTER TEN

KNITTING FOR OTHERS

There are countless organizations that solicit and accept knitted donations. Just google "charity knitting near me" to discover a myriad of groups spreading love through their passion for knitting. Good knitters can knit a hat in an evening. A hat might not seem like much, but if you have ever had the opportunity to donate one, you know how much a hand-knitted item means.

I still see the hats that we handed out at our emergency food cupboard several years ago on the heads of people in the neighborhood. They are treasured. Someone took the time to knit a unique, colorful hat for someone they didn't know. Chemo patients value hats made especially for them that are comfortable as well as beautiful. They look forward to taking off a hot itchy wig and donning a hat made from the softest baby alpaca yarn. Parents of babies in the NICU have told me that a hand-knitted baby blanket is a symbol of hope for them. The prayers of love in every stitch give them the strength to persevere.

Knitting for others is a wonderful ministry. I've seen productive knitters work their way through their stash and produce hundreds of hats. There is no substitute for a hand-knitted item as a way to spread a sense of love and belonging to those who are suffering, feeling neglected or alone. There are enough organizations and patterns to keep us busy for

as long as we can knit. We can knit for veterans, merchant marines, infants, cancer patients, the elderly, animal shelters, prisoners, migrants, children, and those in hospice. The list is practically endless.

If you feel called to this ministry, start by researching organizations that accept knitted donations. Some will have suggested yarns and patterns on their website. Lacy blankets don't work for newborns because their tiny hands and feet can get tangled in the holes. Certain wools are too itchy for chemo caps. Find a pattern and yarn that appeals to you. It might be easier to start with hats or small blankets rather than a complicated teddy bear. Commit to just a few items and give yourself a reasonable deadline. Find an organization that speaks to you. I have a son who serves in the military. Knitting for veterans is important to me so they know how grateful I am for their sacrifice.

A knitting ministry helps spread the love of God in a way that people can see and touch. Another way to spread the love is to teach others to knit for themselves.

Some of the populations that knitting ministries serve may not be able to learn to knit. Obviously, animals in shelters can't knit, hospice patients are too sick to knit, and infants are too young, but there are opportunities to share the craft at home-less shelters, veterans' centers, food cupboards, children's centers, or any place where people gather.

Start by placing yourself in a conspicuous area, and begin knitting. Be sure to have extra needles and yarn in your bag that would be appropriate for a new knitter. It may take a few times knitting at the same place to establish some trust before someone wanders over and shows some interest. I usually work on a project like a simple hat. Hats are great new knitter projects because, unlike a scarf, they can be completed fairly quickly and the new knitter learns the four basic skills: knitting, purling, increasing, and decreasing.

I knit at the emergency food cupboard. People show up and choose food off a "menu" that is generated by the food cupboard. This way, clients get what they like rather than a bag of food chosen by someone else. Once they fill out the menu, they settle in to wait for their order. I station myself at one of the tables and knit. The act of knitting changes everything. It brings a sense of calm, makes the space feel more like a home than a church basement, and it invites conversation. What are you making? How do you do that? Who are you making it for? Eventually this evolves into an opportunity to teach. I offer them the needles and say, "Would you like to try knitting a few stitches? I'll show you how." With some encouragement, they take me up on it. The next week, they knit a few more stitches, and a few more after that, and soon they want their own needles and yarn. They are hooked.

When we teach others to knit, they experience the same benefits that we experience. As their confidence grows, they become the new teachers, and more people join the knitting group each week while people wait for their food to be assembled. This community of new knitters feels safe talking about their individual situations, and soon the group is offering suggestions to help each other with some of their challenges like transportation issues, child care, and employment.

Knitting transforms the dynamics of a group. It builds community and establishes a context for forging new relationships. After new knitters start experimenting with their craft, the dynamic shifts. I find myself learning different, inventive techniques from the people I was teaching only a few weeks ago. Clara, who had been knitting for a few weeks, heard there were knitters in another city making hats and mittens for their neighbors. The knitters put the finished items in clear waterproof bags and left them in parks with a note offering the set to anyone who wanted it. Clara had mastered the art of knitting hats almost immediately, and now she wanted to learn the secret of knitting mittens. She was on her way. She wanted to leave her creations around in the park across from her house. Her notes would let people know that the hat and mittens were being made by a person from their neighborhood. She wanted to include a flyer to advertise the day, time, and meeting place of the new knitting group. The food cupboard only allowed people to pick up food twice a month, but the knitters were showing up weekly.

Knitting for others is powerful, teaching others to knit is transforming, and both are important. We can figure out our options, understand our limitations, and then decide what makes the most sense. Desiring to give back to others is an impulse to be thankful for, and discovering the best way of giving back can be rewarding and lead us in new directions.

Take Time to Reflect

The Unfinished Afghan

They were saying, "The Lord has risen indeed, and he has appeared to Simon!" Then they told what had happened on the road, and how he had been made known to them in the breaking of the bread.

—Luke 24:34–35

My aunt was knitting an afghan for her granddaughter when she died. She had chosen a chunky brown wool and a diamond pattern. The entire project was crammed into a yellow floral knitting bag along with a small pad of paper with my aunt's precise handwriting, clearly marking the pattern rows she had completed. My cousin Jody came across the bag while she was cleaning out the "yarn closet." Jody knew the afghan was for her daughter, so she sent it to my mother to finish it. It sat for months in the knitting bag. My mother could not bear to take it out. The loss of my Aunt Rose was still raw, and the afghan was a reminder of the loss. We talked about the afghan when I came to visit. I decided to take it home and see what I could do.

I took it out of the bag and laid it on the bed and held it, remembering my aunt and how much I loved her. I pictured my cousin Jody and her daughter Kristin and thought about their loss. This afghan might help Kristin feel the warmth of her grandmother's hug through space and time. I knew I had to finish it. I didn't knit the original diamond pattern. Instead, I knit a basket weave pattern so that Kristin would always know what her grandmother knit and what was knit by someone else. She could touch the stitches made by her grandmother's hands and feel a connection knowing that the afghan was stitched with love that transcends space and time. I finished it. Kristin was thrilled. She could wrap herself in her grandmother's love.

I still have the afghan my grandmother made for me many years ago. I have one of the sweaters she knit as well. I treasure these pieces because they embody her love. I can touch the stitches she touched, feel the fabric she created, and snuggle under the afghan and wear the sweater.

Lent, Holy Week, and Easter are a time for us to be reminded that love doesn't end. These wonderful knitted pieces created for us by our loved ones are visual reminders of the love we enjoyed from them. We recognize their love in the physical gifts just as the disciples recognized the risen Christ in the breaking of the bread. One simple, ordinary act of breaking bread opened their eyes to the reality that love doesn't end.

Now that I am a grandmother, I hope that some of the knitted items I have made for others will be a physical reminder that they are loved. Even when the sweater unravels, the hat gets lost, or the dog chews a hole in the afghan, they will know that the love remains forever.

Reflection Questions

1. What visible reminders of a loved one do you cherish?
2. Do you have any heirloom knitting projects?
3. How do you express your love through knitting?

The Gift

As we work together with him, we urge you also not to accept the grace of God in vain.

—*2 Corinthians 6:1*

Fingerless gloves are necessary for knitters who want to keep their hands warm during cold winter days. They can be made rather swiftly out of all types of yarn. I have made them for others, but I lacked a pair myself until one of my knitting friends noticed and knit me a pair with bright green and blue yarn. When I unwrapped the gift, I felt the joy only a knitter can feel when they get something made by another knitter. One of my grandmothers, a meticulous, talented knitter, used to say she would never make me anything because she knew I could knit it myself. She missed the point. Many of us can buy whatever we want or need. Why give a gift if we can just go buy it ourselves?

Gift giving is about so much more than the actual object. It's the thought that goes into it, it's the surprise of the offering, and it's the feeling of being cared for and loved.

Happily, my friend gets it. She knits for knitters. My mother gets it, too. I have a few things she has knit for me, but one of my favorites is a beautiful shawl made from hand-dyed yarn. I love the ethereal way it catches the light and its incredible softness. I can picture her knitting, thinking about me, imagining the garment wrapped around me, a metaphorical hug that exists despite the physical distance between us.

The greatest gift of all is the grace that comes from God. It's freely given, totally undeserved, and changes everything. All we have to do is receive it. Grace is real, grace saves, and grace surrounds us like the shawl, enhancing who we are and helping us become who we are called to be. God's grace is pervasive; we want to experience it, not just believe in it. We do that in community through the sacraments of the church. Each Sunday, we celebrate the Eucharist. We taste and see that God is good, and we recognize the grace that is always present and available. The communal worship reminds us of this gift from God that sustains us and gives us courage to live a Christian life. Grace, the gift we can't give ourselves, the gift we don't deserve, is the one gift we need.

Reflection Questions

1. Where do you see God's grace in your life?
2. How do you say yes to God's grace?
3. What part does the Eucharist play in your spiritual life?

Community

Q. How is the Church described in the Bible?

A. The Church is described as the Body of which Jesus Christ is the Head and of which all baptized persons are members. It is called the People of God, the New Israel, a holy nation, a royal priesthood, and the pillar and ground of truth.

—*Book of Common Prayer, p. 854*

As our spirituality deepens, we look for others to share our experience. Knitters like to come together to encourage each other and use their craft to help others. They enjoy challenging one another, like the group of knitters who decided to knit forty prayer shawls during the forty days of Lent. They accomplished their goal, and on Easter Sunday there were forty prayer shawls in a rainbow of colors draped over the communion rail ready to be blessed. This project pulled the knitters together into a close community.

Then their priest, Donna, was diagnosed with stage four cancer.

Barbara, an older woman, was one of the leaders of the group. She was a beautiful knitter who created sweaters for her grandchildren that sported pictures of their favorite animal or cartoon character. She was also a quilter and had received multiple prizes at the county fair for her appliqué and patchwork designs. She suggested to the knitting group that they spend a week in prayer asking God how they could comfort their priest during the last few months of her life. They agreed.

A week later they got together. Lori, the youngest member of the group and a beginning knitter who had struggled to knit a prayer shawl during the Lenten project, suggested that they knit their priest a prayer shawl. The shawl would travel from person to person, and each knitter would have an opportunity to knit whatever they wanted. They would decide what kind of yarn they would use and how many inches they would knit in the twenty-four-hour timeframe they were allocated. Barbara would take the shawl from person to person and be available to help choose stitch patterns and needle sizes.

A month later, the group stood around admiring the full-length cape they had created. Barbara had knit a collar and sewn silver clasps on one side and added an icord loop to the other side to hold the cape closed. The cape itself was a combination of blues, greens, and purples that blended beautifully like a watercolor painting. It was a true communal creation that showed intention, creativity, and love. When Donna opened the box a month after her diagnosis, she gasped and declared it breathtaking. It was a visual expression of the community she had helped build, and the love that it contained overwhelmed her. She wore it every day until she became bedridden, and then it served as her bedspread. Donna gave thanks for the community of knitters that enabled her to see and feel the love that surrounded her as she completed her life journey.

Reflection Questions

1. How can your knitting connect you with people in your community?
2. What does community mean to you?
3. What project can you initiate to promote community?

CHAPTER ELEVEN

KNITTING THROUGH GRIEF

Jesus began to weep.
—*John 11:35*

Grief is a powerful and unpredictable emotion. The beginning stages of grief can be intense as the feeling tries to break through the wall of denial in the face of tragedy or loss. For the person experiencing the grief, the feeling can be overwhelming and difficult to navigate. One of the challenges is dealing with the emotions of others. I consistently hear from people that they just don't know what to say to someone who is suffering. Often, they parrot platitudes they have heard from others like "God doesn't give you more than you can handle" or "Everything happens for a reason." None of this is helpful to the person who is suffering. Working through grief is not easy, but getting help from those who care about us can really make a difference in our experience.

Watching someone we love grieve is painful. We want to fix it. But we can't, and there are times where there is nothing we can say. So how can we be present to their grief? Let them cry, talk, or be silent. All we have to do is listen, nod, and offer a reassuring touch. Let their grief be heard, especially when it is new.

Our desire to make it better, to fix it, wants to take action. Isn't there something I can do? Actually, there is. We can take over day-to-day chores so they can be free to do the work of grief. We can bring over a meal, put in a load of laundry, make the beds, or clean the kitchen. Completing these everyday activities is calming and reassuring. The stuff of life continues even in the midst of intense emotional pain. When the work is done, we can sit and knit. We can be a non-anxious presence in the midst of the trauma.

Knitting helps us be present while doing something. We can knit our prayers into whatever we are making. A priest mentor and friend, William, was going through a divorce. He was devastated. The loss was too much to bear, and his hope for the latter part of his life to be full of love and companionship was shattered. In his retirement years, he had resigned himself to being alone. His grief was palpable, and he expressed it by describing himself in a very dark place. There was no consolation in the early days of his separation. He hung onto his faith even though God seemed unreachable from the depth of his sadness.

I visited him occasionally and listened to his pain. I was desperate to do something. I started to knit him a stole. I found two skeins of yarn that were made up of a mixture of different types of white and gold yarn. There were thin strands the color of coffee full of cream, bulky strands of antique ivory, and bright white wool mixed with metallic gold yarn that reflected the light. I prayed as hard as I could, asking God to heal his pain as I knit him this Easter stole.

William spent Lent that year wandering through the wilderness of his grief, lost and directionless. I gave him his stole on Holy Saturday. He was touched by the gift, but I saw the sadness in his eyes. This Easter would not bring him the personal resurrection I had prayed for. It was too soon. Grief takes the time it takes, and we can't make it go away any faster just because we want it to.

Grief demands its time and if we don't acknowledge it, it will find a way to express itself. A man whose wife had died of cancer a few months ago called me because he wanted to talk.

When we got together, he ranted about a contractor that was doing renovations on his house. He was incredibly angry. I was puzzled. Why did he need a priest to complain about his contractor? I realized he was angry about the death of his wife and he was looking for a way to express his grief.

A year later, I noticed that William had begun to return to his old self. He started laughing again and became interested in what was going on around him. A few years after that, he fell in love and remarried. William told me how much it meant for him to receive the white and gold stole I had made for him even though he was still in the midst of his grief. It was the sign of hope, the symbol of resurrection that he needed in the midst of his sorrow.

If we knit for someone who is grieving, we have to let go of our expectations. How they react to the gift is dependent on where they are in the grieving process, and that process is different for everyone. The gift may sit in a box or be thrown into a closet, but it is there, an expression of our love. The presence of the gift does make a difference even if the person is not ready to engage it or us. Give the gift and let it go. The prayers we prayed with each stitch are enough.

Knitting through our own grief can be healing, but we need to be ready. My maternal grandmother died when I was twenty-five. My first child was four months old, and we had just returned from visiting her. I was heartbroken. This woman's love for me had been unconditional. We were connected in a special way, and I couldn't imagine life without her. I wanted to share the joys of motherhood with her. I cried in the restroom at the funeral home while I nursed my son, grieving all the moments she would miss with me and her great-grandson. There was nothing I could do to make myself feel better. This was the first time I had experienced a significant loss, and grief was new to me.

I found it exhausting nursing an infant, not getting enough sleep, dealing with hormones, and trying to grieve a central figure in my life. Three months after she died, my aunts shipped me my grandmother's knitting stash. It was the size of a large moving box and was full of needles, yarn, and pattern books. Had this box shown up any earlier, I would have put it away because it would have been too painful for me to open. But now, after a few months, I wanted something of hers to hold to remind me of her.

I went through her stash like a forensic detective. This skein of yarn was left over from the sweater she knit for one of the grandchildren, and here was yarn left over from the afghan she knit for me. I remember teasing her about these pea green plastic knitting needles. There were no unfinished objects. She was too frugal. There were only her tools and leftover yarn. Her knitting legacy had been passed to me. I treasure those pea green plastic needles. I keep them in the tapestry case that I had seen her use all my life. I transferred my UFOs onto her needles, and every time I was able to sit down and knit, I could almost feel her hands guiding me like she had when I learned how to knit. I would knit and cry until one day I just sat and knit. The needles changed from a source of sadness to a treasured memory.

Today, over thirty years later, I still use her needles to knit for my grandchildren. She was my role model for how to be a grandmother. She gave me her full attention when we were together. I wasn't aware of the power of being fully present, fully available to another person at the time. Now I understand. My children wonder why their children are better behaved with Grandma. The reason is because my entire attention is focused on them. I don't have to worry about making dinner, doing huge loads of laundry, grocery shopping, taking children to their activities, and all the tasks that keep young families busy. I can just sit and read story after story and play pretend games.

The best way to engage grief is by being fully present to it when we can. This is true for our own grief and for the grief of others. Knitting during the experience can help with the healing process. The sweater I knit that absorbed my tears after my grandmother died still sits in a drawer. It's made of purple mohair, and it's itchy if I wear it next to my skin. It's one of my most prized possessions.

Take Time to Reflect

Grieving a Loss

And I say, "It is my grief that the right hand of the Most High has changed."

—*Psalm 77:10*

Grieving a loss is hard work. It can start with a divorce, job loss, or the death of a loved one, and suddenly we feel like we are carrying a fifty-pound bag of sand that we can't put down. We try to find a more comfortable way of carrying the bag, so we shift it around, holding it in front and then carrying it on the side, finally heaving it up onto our shoulders. Regardless of where we put it, it weighs us down and tires us out.

My mother's grief after my father died dragged her down. After the funeral, she returned to her home in Florida alone to find a new way of being in the world. She was devastated by her loss, and she just didn't know what to do with herself. Her best friend of over fifty years, who I called Aunt Rose, telephoned her every morning to check in from her home in Connecticut. One of the few things they enjoyed talking about was their various knitting projects.

During one of their morning phone conversations, they decided to knit the Great American Aran Afghan together. Rose bought some red yarn, my mother went with a light green, and they started to knit. The Great American Aran Afghan is made up of twenty-five different square patterns designed by twenty-five different designers. They began a two-person knit-along. They picked a square and started to knit. Each morning they would share their progress, discuss their challenges with the pattern, and my mother would talk about her loss.

This went on for months. I was intrigued and bought the pattern book and completed a square. The patterns were interesting, challenging, and captivating, thereby creating a beautiful distraction. My mother knit her way through her grief, creating a small tear in the sandbag of sadness, allowing some sand to fall away and lighten her load. The companionship with her longtime friend, paired with the all-encompassing Great American Aran Afghan patterns, was the right prescription for healing.

The finished afghan became an outward expression of my mother's grief. She had poured all of herself into the creation. There were memories in the patterns of when she and Rose had struggled to understand the directions or when the square was too small or when they had to start over.

I will always be grateful to my Aunt Rose for being present to my mother's grief. When we grieve, we need a witness. We don't need someone forcing us to ignore our feelings or move on too quickly. Grief needs to be acknowledged, and we can't do all our grieving alone. Even though Aunt Rose was over a thousand miles away, she was still present almost tangibly through the knitting project. We can feel God's healing love through the presence of others, especially when they are open to hearing our pain. What a gift when a friend asks, "How are you?" and really wants to know.

The heavy burden of grief may diminish over time, but it never fully goes away. We work to make it a manageable size, one that we can carry without struggling. Sometimes it's quiet, sometimes it demands attention, but it's there twenty-four hours a day and seven days a week, sapping our energy. Aunt Rose and my mother took the energy that was seeping away and put it into their afghans. They transformed the weight of grief into popcorn stitches and cables, forming a healing cocoon of yarn.

Reflection Questions

1. How do you carry your grief?
2. Who has been present to your grief?
3. What would you knit to work through your grief?

The Impractical Shawl

"Be still and know that I am God."

—*Psalm 46:10*

I know my knitting preferences. I don't like knitting with lace weight yarn on small needles, but there are times when a knitter has to make an exception. I was perusing the yarn inventory at Sew Green, a store where knitters donate their unwanted stash, and I found several skeins of Rowan's Kid Silk Haze in a bright white. The yarn has the consistency of cotton candy, and one strand is barely detectable on the skin. I was drawn to it. What could I make out of this cloud of softness? After searching Ravelry, I found the perfect pattern by Kit Hutchins—the Mohair Bias Loop. This pattern uses size 10½ needles to create an airy fabric knit on the bias to form a seamless loop that can either be worn as a long scarf, twisted double to form a cowl, or just stretched over the shoulders to create a translucent wrap. One of the pictures shows the shoulder wrap over a wedding gown. The bright white lace weight yarn was meant for this pattern.

I discovered it took focused attention to poke the size 10½ needle into the spiderweb-thin yarn and make a stitch. Instead of being discouraged, I decided the project would be perfect for prayerful knitting. As the stitches accumulated, I noticed how the delicate yarn turned into a feathery fabric that seemed to float on the air. There was barely any weight to it. Every day for weeks I poked the huge needle into the fragile loop like I was knitting in slow motion. Each movement was measured. I had to look directly at the needle, separate out a stitch, and then bring it close to the end of the needle so I could fit the tip of the needle into the stitch, being careful to create a tension that wasn't too loose. It was mesmerizing. The world fell away, and it was just me, the repetitive calming motions of knitting, and the ethereal cloud of feathery fabric.

I was grateful for the project because it helped me stay grounded as I watched one of my friends struggle with stage four brain cancer. I went to see her in the hospital. Although I knew there was nothing to be done except be present to her suffering, I blurted out that I wanted to do something. She responded, you can give me a hug. I hugged her. She told me she was having trouble discerning God's presence in her life at this difficult moment.

She believed that God loved her, but she wanted to feel it. She wanted something beyond the human touch of her loved ones.

I wrapped up the white Mohair Bias Loop that I had just finished and brought it to her in the hospital. When she extracted it from the box, she gasped at the exquisiteness of fabric and said, "What is it?" I took it from her, pulled it over her head, positioned it on her shoulders, and said, "Feel the love of God." She wore it every day until she died.

Reflection Questions

1. What things help you feel close to God?
2. How do you use your knitting to comfort others?
3. What have you knit with lace weight yarn?

Audio Books

Pay heed, Job, listen to me; be silent, and I will speak.

—Job 33:31

The invention of audiobooks is a game changer. Folding laundry, emptying the dishwasher, and knitting seventeen inches of stockinette pattern can be riveting with a psychological thriller. When I first discovered audiobooks, I was listening to them as often as I could. I couldn't wait to go to the grocery store so I could listen in the car, sometimes sitting in the parking lot for twenty minutes until I could make myself turn it off. Soon I was walking the dog, making the bed, cleaning the house, knitting, and doing all my chores while listening to a book. I was racking up the titles, and my friends were astounded when they found out that I had "read" almost all the books on the best sellers list. But in reality, I had quit reading.

I knew it was bad when my husband came home one day and asked me if I had walked the dog. I couldn't remember. I checked the steps on my watch. I had over fifteen thousand steps so I'm sure I did walk the dog, but I realized I was living in another world even though I was walking in this one. I had entered the world of my audiobook. This was the equivalent of binge-watching entire seasons of TV shows, but since I was getting my chores done, no one really objected. Plus my earphones were hidden by my long hair, so no one noticed what I was doing until they tried to start a conversation and I didn't respond.

I found that my new habit had effectively shut out my inner thoughts. Walking had been my way to process, but now it was full of narration and I was unaware of anything else. I began to miss aspects of the outdoors, the smell of the rain-soaked earth, the leaves changing color, the footprints of the twin deer that lived in the woods, and the joy of the dog as she sniffed her favorite spots. I had to limit my listening to books so I could listen to myself.

There is nothing wrong with sitting down for an hour or two to knit and listen to a good book. I learned to set limits in advance and stick to them. Now I knit from 2:00 to 4:00 and then I will move to a different activity. I make sure I have time to listen to myself. I know it's important to be present to my inner life and especially to my feelings. What was I trying to block out by staying busy listening to my books? Was I avoiding something? The answer was a resounding yes. I was avoiding the grief I was feeling over my dad's death. It was easier to distract myself than to allow myself to feel the sadness. I had to learn how to balance feeling my grief and escaping from my grief. Both are necessary.

There are days when I knit with the book and then days when I cry and knit in silence, remembering my Dad and giving thanks for his life.

Reflection Questions

1. Is the TV or radio on all the time in your house?
2. Do you always listen to music while you exercise?
3. Are you present to your inner life and feelings?

CHAPTER TWELVE

STASH EXAMEN

I have a yarn stash. When the children left home, I took over a bedroom, which we refer to as my hobby room. It is filled with project bags, yarn, needles, tape measures, jars of buttons, fabric, and notions of all kinds. When we rented out the house for a year, this was the one room that remained closed to the renters. I had to decide what unfinished objects to take with me, and I agonized for days over my choices. Leaving forced me to spend some time reflecting on my overabundance of yarn.

Reflecting on our stash is an excellent way to discover our preferences about our possessions. Often these preferences spill over into our spiritual lives.

Wait, what if you don't have a stash? What if you only have enough yarn to finish your current project? I can think of several reasons for this. You are a new knitter and you are still learning. The idea of buying more yarn is overwhelming. You are organized, and having more material than what you are using causes anxiety. You are in the minority of knitters. Be grateful. Skip this section and keep knitting.

For those of us who have a yarn stash, the first step in this reflection process is to let go of any judgments about our stash and make some simple observations. What is in your stash? This may take some time to figure out depending on how large the stash is. The best way to answer this question is to catalog every bit of yarn. Choose a method that works for you. You could make a list, start a spreadsheet, or enter your stash in Ravelry.

Ravelry is a powerful online tool that allows you to track your stash, maintain an online library of your patterns and knitting books, post your projects, search for patterns, host groups of knitters with different interest, and lots more. If you haven't signed up, do it. Even if you are not technical, it's easy to use and you can find tutorials online. Listing your stash on Ravelry will open up more options as you make decisions about your stash. Be sure to include the following information: the name of the yarn, what it is made out of (wool, cotton, etc.), the quantity (grams and yards), the color, the dye lot, the weight, the gauge, if it is earmarked for a project or being used to make a project, where you purchased the yarn, and its current location.

Now that you know what's in your stash, you can make some observations. What do you notice first? When my friend Sarah did this exercise, she noticed that she cared the most about where she had purchased the yarn. Her stash was more a catalog of her travels than a list of yarn. She had gotten the white wool that smelled like lanolin on a knitting cruise through Australia and New Zealand, the indigo lace yarn at the Sheep and Wool Festival in Vermont, and the cashmere yarn out in Washington state. Each set of yarn held memories of the events she had attended.

Another friend noticed that her stash was made up of yarn purchased for magazine patterns that she loved. When her magazine arrived in the mail, she would spend time looking at patterns until she found one she liked, and then she would be on the hunt for the yarn. She would look for the exact yarn in the same color as the picture, no substitutes allowed. Sometimes this required her to buy internationally, but she enjoyed the process of finding and obtaining the yarn. She was buying yarn for four sweaters a year. She was barely completing two a year along with knitting gifts and her knitting for the homeless shelter. Her closet was full of project bags for sweaters that she had already forgotten.

Terri went to yarn stores for retail therapy. Whenever she had a bad day or felt depressed, she would wander into her favorite yarn store and feel the skeins until she found one she liked. Sometimes it was the texture and sometimes it was the color that would attract her. Her stash was a variety of mostly single skeins of yarn.

What is our stash telling us?

My stash is mostly unfinished objects on the needles. I have one bag of yarn that I bought to make a coat. It was not the recommended yarn. The gauge worked for the pattern, but the swatch was soft and stretchy. I could foresee the coat stretching until it reached the ground, so the yarn sits in my closet, all sixteen skeins. My stash tells me that I like to start projects. Once I learn a pattern or stare too long at the deep red yarn that I always seem to pick, I get bored and want to move to something different.

Asking questions about our stash can help us understand the positive and negative characteristics of our preferences. These are clues that can help us figure out what we might need to be aware of in other areas of our lives. Sarah's stash holds her travel memories. When she knits from her stash, it brings her back to the places that she visited. Sarah is back inside the yarn store in Scotland recalling her conversation with the owner and her decision to buy the worsted weight wool rather than the lace weight silk. When Sarah spent time reflecting on her stash, she realized that she spent most of her knitting time living in the past. She was barely aware of the time she spent knitting and often made simple knitting mistakes because she was not present to her knitting. Her prayer time was similar. She would start out in the moment, but within seconds she had journeyed back to a pleasant memory and time would pass unnoticed. Sarah was not cultivating her awareness of the presence of God in the moment. This discovery unveiled the reason for her frustration with her prayer practice.

Terri's stash was made up of single skeins of expensive luxurious yarns. There was a skein of cashmere and linen the color of a fine merlot, a baby alpaca skein the shade of a blue bird's egg, and a brilliant orange silk that appeared to be perpetually bathed in sunlight. They were like a collection of Faberge eggs. Terri's reflection revealed that she was purchasing yarn as a quick fix for her feelings of anxiety. She did have several projects in her stash that she was actively knitting, but she was collecting the single skeins without any thought of how she might use them. The collection was growing and becoming a source of anxiety for her as she reflected on the amount of money it represented. Terri spent her prayer time praying for others. People asked her to pray for them and their loved ones. They told her the stories of each person in great detail, outlining their cancer treatments, their setbacks, their tragedies, their losses, and Terri would soak it up like a sponge. Knitting was her happy place, and luxury yarns reminded her that there was something beyond suffering.

Her spiritual advisor was a knitter. She suggested that Terri start knitting with the luxury yarn in her stash and pray for herself. Initially, Terri felt uncomfortable with this idea. It seemed selfish. Her advisor reassured her that we all need prayers, and there was nothing wrong with asking for God's help. Terri needed to learn how to be present to people's suffering without taking on their pain. The more Terri prayed for herself, the more she was able to be present to others. She knit a scarf for herself out of the baby alpaca. She knit a few more scarfs from her luxury yarn stash and gave them away as gifts. When other knitters admired a particular skein, she would pluck it off the shelf and give it to them. Terri felt lighter, less anxious, as her stash disappeared. She still visited the yarn store when she was anxious, but she didn't feel compelled to buy anything. She was content to browse until she needed a new project. She thanked God for the help she was getting through her prayers for herself, and she continued praying for others.

My stash tells me I like distractions. I'm like a squirrel when it comes to knitting. I see something and I run toward it until I see something else, and then I change direction. I start a project and work on it for a while, and then I see a picture in a magazine or someone else's project and I abandon what I'm doing. I will go back and knit on a project that has been hibernating, but something has to compel me. I bought a large amount of yarn to make a floor-length bathrobe with a train. I knit about fourteen inches and then stuffed it all in a bag. A few years later, I was at a knitting group and the woman across from me was knitting a pattern that reminded me of the bathrobe. It was the very same bathrobe that was languishing in my closet. She was pregnant and she was knitting it to wear in the hospital. I wanted to leave the knitting group, go home, and start knitting the bathrobe.

This squirrel behavior pattern has expressed itself in my spiritual life. I have a collection of different prayer books, rosaries, finger labyrinths, and spiritual reading material. I start with one prayer book and then exchange it for another within a few weeks. I go from labyrinths to rosaries to chanting psalms to morning prayer. I excuse my behavior by claiming I was bored. Changing a spiritual practice every few weeks hindered my desire to cultivate a deeper relationship with God. Using different tools became a distraction. I was dipping my toe into multiple practices without ever submerging myself. I discovered that I was susceptible to distractions that caused me to have more than a few unfinished objects in my stash as well as a superficial spiritual practice.

Spending a year away from my stash when I had the opportunity to live in Europe was enlightening. The problem was my luggage was extremely limited and I could only choose a few projects to bring with me. Limiting my choices turned out to be a gift. It enabled me to stick with a knitting project, a prayer book, and a practice. It made me persevere when I became uncomfortable. In the past, whenever I felt challenged, I would put down the knitting project and start something else. The instructions want a short row shaping on the shoulders using a clip and turn method? What's that? The project goes back in the bag, and it's on to something else.

Eventually all my projects had progressed to a point where the next step was challenging. I had no choice but to figure it out. Most knitters know there are plenty of resources available to help with knitting. All it took was asking my new friends from my knitting group for help or watching a few YouTube videos when I was alone, and I was able to tackle every challenge. I felt the joy of making progress.

We lived in a small apartment surrounded by the objects we were able to fit in two suitcases. The lack of possessions was freeing. There were no distractions. I committed to saying Morning Prayer and writing down one verse from the Psalms every day. When I did my spiritual knitting, I would start by saying the Psalm verse and gradually trail off and just knit in the presence of God.

I finished five hibernating knitting projects in quick succession. My husband saw me admiring them and remarked, "I thought you never finished anything."

Once we reveal the secrets of our stash, we can make choices about it. Terri decided to use her luxury yarn as gifts. Some skeins she knits, other skeins she gives away. Some she sells online. She let go of the yarn and released its potential. We all have the choice to let go of yarn or to keep it. I went through my stash and considered each project. Would I ever finish the pink leg warmers I had started six years ago when I was taking ballet? I had abandoned the project after I discovered a post online about a mistake in the traveling cable stitch pattern. I couldn't find the pattern to a blue sock I was knitting that looked like ocean waves. Did I really want to tear out the wavy pattern sock and start over with a different pattern? Was I going to try a fifth time to knit a lacy shawl out of the sticky mohair yarn?

I gathered up those projects and took them to a ministry in Rochester called Sew Green. Sew Green takes donations of fabric, yarn, thread, needles—anything to do with sewing, knitting, and crocheting. They resell people's donations at a small fraction of the original price. They make crafting affordable. The Rev. Georgia Carney, who started Sew Green, told me we are a nation of hoarders. As I packed up a large part of my stash, I knew she was right. I was embarrassed by the amount of yarn and projects I had started and abandoned. After I dropped off my load at Sew Green, I felt unencumbered. I hadn't realized how this accumulation of stuff was weighing me down. The next day, there was an ad on social media enticing people to come to Sew Green and see the latest donation of beautiful yarn.

The spiritual life is about letting go. Letting go of our physical possessions can help us let go of our emotional and spiritual baggage.

Take Time to Reflect
Celebrate the Milestones

. . . make my joy complete: be of the same mind, having the same love, being in full accord and of one mind.

—*Philippians 2:2*

I tend to live in the future. I start thinking about unfinished objects I might attack next or what new knitting project I've seen recently in a magazine or on Ravelry as I'm weaving in the ends of the current project.

Completing a project is a cue to take some time for reflection. First, we should celebrate. Congratulations are in order. We have finished something, and finishing is an accomplishment. It is a mile marker on the journey. We have completed this section of the path so we should stop, enjoy, and mark the moment. We do this for birthdays since they are a natural milestone in time. We celebrate our lives, we give thanks, we reflect on the past and set goals for the future. We make meaning of our experiences.

Reflection is essential for growth, but it takes time and intention. Reflection is critical for a spiritual life, and sometimes our knitting projects can provide a metaphor that helps in our reflection.

Anna was a monogamous knitter. She diligently worked on one project at a time, and when she finished she would wait a month or two before she bought yarn for a new project. She recently joined a knitting group and as she knit on a sweater for her nephew, she watched Laura working on a multicolored lace shawl made up of twenty-four doll-size skeins of yarn that came packaged in a floral box with a cellophane window. The packaging made the yarn look like a box of macarons from Paris. Each week, Anna watched Laura take a tiny skein of fine lace yarn out of the box and incorporate it into the shawl. This week the skein was pink and it could have been mistaken for cotton candy. Anna spent her time in the group watching Laura and coveting the yarn.

After a few weeks of salivating over the pink cotton candy, the lemon yellow, and the mint green skeins, Anna broke down and bought the yarn. For some of us, this would be a natural turn of events, but for Anna, buying this yarn created anxiety. She was conflicted. Do I finish the sweater for my nephew or start the shawl? She started the shawl. As she wrestled with the pattern, she remembered that she had tried knitting lace garments in the past and she didn't like lace. She couldn't "read" the knitting and she wasn't sure if she had made a mistake, and if she had made a mistake, she didn't know how to correct it. The fine yarn turned into a bird's nest when she tried to take it out. Her knitting became a chore, then a punishment for her impulse buy. She stopped going to the knitting group, stuffed both projects into her closet, and pushed any thoughts of knitting out of her mind.

Regular reflection can help prevent these moments. Examining our actions, motivations, and thought processes can lead us to know ourselves better and prevent the pitfalls that come when we operate with a lack of self-awareness. Anna was attracted to the uniqueness of the yarn and its packaging. The macaron-colored skeins were an indulgent treat, just like the cookies she had seen in French bakeries. Reflective curiosity about this yarn may have helped Anna realize that what she really needed was to take time to care for herself. Anna was a single woman who paid attention to everyone else's needs first.

She didn't think about her own needs. Impulsively buying yarn for a project that she wouldn't enjoy knitting was proof.

It took a few months before Anna was ready to look at the projects stuffed in her closet. She sat with them in her lap and asked herself what she could learn from each one. She finished her nephew's sweater and gave the twenty-two intact macaron-like skeins to Laura. Another few months went by and Laura presented Anna with a completed macaron shawl, which became Anna's visual reminder of the power of reflection.

A consistent prayer practice creates new levels of awareness in our lives. We see things differently, and it causes us to ask questions. What is God calling us to do?

Reflection Questions

1. What new observations have you made about your life?
2. What questions have come up in your prayer practice?
3. What is God asking you to do?

Stash Examination

Do not store up for yourselves treasures on earth, where moth and rust consume and where thieves break in and steal; but store up for yourselves treasures in heaven, where neither moth nor rust consumes and where thieves do not break in and steal. For where your treasure is, there your heart will be also.

—Matthew 6:19–21

Living a spiritual life requires self-examination. What are the right questions? What aspects of our lives do we need to look at? Is it how we spend our time? Is it how we manage our relationships? What are our priorities? What might need to change?

Examining our yarn stash can be a good way to look at our priorities. What we stash and how we stash is an interesting metaphor for life.

My stash is mostly projects in various stages of development. I don't have any yarn in my stash that is not already earmarked for a project, but at last count I had twenty-three projects on the needles. I like to have choices, but when does it become too many? I need to examine everything I have and then prioritize and focus. Otherwise, nothing gets done. I can tell when I'm really out of control or when I'm trying to avoid the work I need to do when I keep buying more yarn and patterns for even more projects.

In the course of one month, I bought a lopi yarn sweater kit, yarn for a pullover t-shirt made of cashmere and linen, and yarn for a sweater made of three lace weight yarns held together, which of course made the sweater very expensive. These purchases were made even though I knew I had over fifteen projects already on needles. What am I avoiding? I'm sure it's the laborious work of writing, finding more grants for my inner-city church, or maybe even tackling the mess in the attic.

I like starting a project. After the initial excitement, it gets hard. There are inches and inches of boring stockinette that need to get done, or I have to sit with a chart in my lap and try to remember what the downward sloping line with a misshapen star in the corner represents.

Examination is a time of discernment, a time to reorder our lives and bring our priorities back to God. Where is God calling us at this time? This is the question we can ask ourselves when we sit down to pray. The answer comes over time. The same thought keeps popping into our heads until it becomes top of mind. We can offer it up to others and see what they think. Is this discernment coming from God or is it coming from somewhere else? Is this what God wants for me or is it what I want for myself or is it what others want for me?

Discerning priorities is like looking at a wall full of yarn. Many of my knitter friends have bought yarn just because they like it. They may have thought at the time, this would make a nice sweater or possibly a shawl, but they didn't have a pattern in mind. A stash of yarn not only holds potential, our stash holds memories. Discernment starts with understanding where we've been and where we are now. The blue mohair is from your favorite yarn shop in town. You went there with a new knitting friend who had just moved into the area and you couldn't resist. The forest green merino wool came from the interesting woman who was actually spinning the yarn during a festival that you stumbled across on your anniversary trip to New England. The yarn causes us to think back to different times in our lives. What was good about that time, what needed changing? Examining our lives can help us unlock our potential. Pick one area to change, one relationship to improve, one new activity to start, or one new volunteer opportunity. Grab the yarn from the stash and unlock its potential.

I have decided to work consistently on the pullover made with the three lace weights yarns and stop avoiding my more challenging work. This will involve learning how to knit Japanese short rows, but I'm up for the challenge.

Reflection Questions

1. What does your stash tell you about your priorities?
2. Pick something from your stash. What potential is waiting to be uncovered?
3. What small change can you make in your life that will deepen your relationship with God?

CHAPTER THIRTEEN
KNITTING THROUGH LENT

Lent is an excellent time to begin or renew a spiritual practice. At the Ash Wednesday liturgy, the priest invites us to a holy Lent, laying out ways we can live into renewing our relationship with God:

> I invite you, therefore, in the name of the Church, to the observance of a holy Lent, by self-examination and repentance; by prayer, fasting, and self-denial; and by reading and meditating on God's holy Word.
>
> —*Book of Common Prayer, p. 265*

Lent is a time to stop, reflect on our own lives. We can think about what is going well and where we might want to make changes. What temptations exist in our lives? What distracts us from our call to follow Jesus? What questions continue to come up in our prayer life?

Lent is an opportunity to spend time reflecting on our priorities as we prepare ourselves for Easter. What needs to be resurrected in our lives? Where are we looking for new life? Questions like these can guide us through the forty-day journey of Lent as we commit to spending time in self-examination, prayer, and studying scripture. Knitting an inch per day is a way to spend time with God and to have a visual record of the commitment.

What follows is a guide to knitting through Lent. You can knit through Lent on your own, or you could gather up some friends and start a Lenten Knit-Along. You can keep knitting on your chosen project, create the forty-inch Lenten cowl following the pattern included in this book, or develop your own pattern. The idea is to commit to forty days of knitting which will enable time for reflection and prayer.

The Project Preparation

The Lenten Knit-Along project is a forty-inch cowl. The idea is to knit one inch a day for forty days while praying.

1. Choose a yarn. Any yarn will do. How about some yarn hanging out in your stash?
2. Choose the size needles recommended for your yarn. This can be found on the ball band or just experiment until the knitted fabric is what you want.
3. Cast on twelve stitches, knit at least twelve rows, and check your gauge. You want to know two things: how many stitches per inch and how many rows per inch. Since the goal is to knit one inch per day, you may want to pick a yarn that is a worsted weight to bulky weight.

Example

I have chosen a handspun yarn that has been in my stash for a long time. I am using size 8 needles, and I plan on casting on forty-eight stitches (there are a lot of stitch patterns that use a multiple of eight stitches). After finishing my gauge swatch, I know I will be knitting four rows a day (this equals one inch of length). This seems doable. Once I have knit the forty inches, I plan on joining the two ends together for a wraparound cowl that will be forty inches long by twelve inches wide.

Some Additional Things to Consider as You Prepare

1. Invite your friends to join you so you can encourage one another.
2. Think about what time of day will you sit down to pray (knit/crochet)? What might get in the way? Do you have a backup time?
3. Where will you sit down to pray? How will you prevent interruptions?
4. What will you do if you go several days without praying? How will you get back on track?

Committing to something for forty days doesn't seem like much until the newness wears off and all the demands of everyday life start encroaching on your designated prayer time. Suddenly it's been three days since you picked up your project. As each day goes by, it gets harder and harder to restart, and there is the abandoned project on your bedside table mocking you.

Trust me, I've been there. Here are some hints that may help:

- Don't make your daily goals too time consuming. If you commit to too many rows or too much time, you could be setting yourself up for failure. It's consistency that's important. Better to do sixty seconds per day of prayer than nothing.
- Figure out a strategy for getting back to your prayer practice. Find a prayer partner that will encourage you. It's not about being perfect, it's about being able to restart.
- Don't try to catch up if you fall behind. Depending on how many days you have missed, catching up can become overwhelming. If you are following a pattern that will take you forty days to complete, don't try to knit two days' worth. Just pick up where you left off and do one day's worth of knitting. There is still time to complete your project after Easter.
- Find other knitters that will support you and help you get back on track. Remember, no guilt—any daily practice is

difficult. Have you ever gone to bed without brushing your teeth? It happens, we just don't want it to keep happening.

The Project

Remember, this is a spiritual exercise. The purpose is not to knit a beautiful cowl. If you want to knit a beautiful cowl, go find a pattern, buy some yarn, and have at it. This knitting project is a visual way to track your prayer time. The idea is to spend time knitting and praying for forty days during Lent. If you are a knitter who carefully follows patterns, this can be an opportunity to create your own pattern. You can decide each day what stitch you want to knit and why. Stitch patterns can become spiritual metaphors.

Take Time to Reflect

Ash Wednesday: Start with the End in Mind

Remember that you are dust and to dust you shall return.

—*Book of Common Prayer, p. 286*

One of my favorite sweaters is a black ski sweater with hearts and snowflakes on the yoke, a smaller white snowflake pattern on the bottom, and flecks of white throughout the black body. I knit it during ski vacations sitting in front of the fire delighting in the intricate pattern of black and white yarn. The directions were impeccable, and when I sewed the sleeves to the body of the sweater, the snowflake pattern on the sleeves matched the snowflake pattern on the yoke perfectly.

Imagine my horror when a friend asked me about a hole they noticed in the snowflake sweater. My first thought was, after all those hours I spent knitting and now it was starting to unravel? Of course, I immediately thought about patching it, but this experience reminded me that nothing lasts forever, not the sweater and not us.

On my first Ash Wednesday as a priest, a woman brought her adorable eighteen-month-old daughter to the communion rail to receive ashes. There I was, my thumb pressed into the soft pale skin of her forehead making a splotchy sign of the cross, ashes falling onto her perky little nose, her large blue eyes focused on mine as I said, "Remember that you are dust and to dust you shall return." The contrast between the words I was saying and the young child in front of me was a liturgical wake-up call. The reminder that we are dust had a way of altering my priorities, conjuring up an attitude of thanksgiving for even the smallest things like feeling the sun on my skin, tasting the sweetness of a newly picked strawberry, and singing silly songs with young children.

Sometimes, we experience this when a loved one dies, but we are usually too overcome with grief to think about how we might respond to the idea of our own mortality. Ash Wednesday gives us an opportunity to really reflect on the priorities of our own lives unencumbered by grief. It is also an invitation to repentance. Repentance is about turning back toward God. Each year, I ask myself, what keeps me from God? What do I need to change in my life?

Embracing my mortality has changed my priorities. Relationships come first, and my relationship with God is paramount. I chose the seed stitch to start my cowl, not just because it makes a nice border, but because it represents potential. God is always sowing seeds that will take root in us.

What will be my new beginning this year?

Reflection Questions

1. What keeps me from God?
2. What gets in the way of deepening my relationships with God?
3. What do I need to change in my life?
4. How will I begin?

Dark Night of the Soul

I tell you, even though he will not get up and give him anything because he is his friend, at least because of his persistence he will get up and give him whatever he needs.

—Luke 11:8

Spiritual darkness happens to all of us. We may experience a sense of being disconnected from God. We may want to abandon our practice. It's not always possible to know why we may be experiencing a spiritual dryness. Sometimes a crisis in our lives can precipitate questions that undermine our faith.

As a chaplain in the hospital, the most common question I encountered from people who were in crisis consisted of one word, *Why?* Many of their other questions could be answered— the who, what, and where of a tragedy—but the why could not. The underlying question is, Why would God let this happen? Why didn't God intervene? Why did this person live and this person die? All of us agonize over these questions that we cannot answer. The "why" question can be the door to doubt.

Tina knew she wanted to dance for as long as she could remember. Her family told stories about how she had started to react to music as a tiny baby. She seemed unable to lie still when music was playing, and she started dance classes at three. By the time she was ten years old, she was dancing with the high school girls. Her long legs and willowy arms were perfect for ballet. Soon she was dancing the lead at recitals, until she fell. It was as if her legs collapsed out from under her. Her fall resulted in a broken femur. Was it a freak accident? No one wanted to believe that this young athlete could be ill. She belonged to a church that delighted in her gift of dance. They prayed for her at every service and in their own personal prayers. There had to be an explanation for her fall. There was.

Tina had brittle bone disease. It wasn't life threatening, but the doctor advised her to stop dancing. This was like telling Tina to stop breathing. She needed to be angry at someone so she became angry at God and the congregation. Their prayers were useless, she told the congregation. The one thing in her life that gave her joy had been taken away because of this disease. Where was God? What good was prayer? Not one person could give her a satisfactory answer. Her priest told her to keep praying. We don't always get what we want, the priest said, but we get what we need. Tina's childhood faith was no match for this crisis. Her disappointment was like a guest that had overstayed its welcome and wouldn't leave.

The older people continued to pray for Tina. They surrounded her with their love. They sat silently with her while her leg healed. They read to her, they played games with her, they helped her with her school work, and they listened to her. The consistent love of the visitors from her church penetrated her dark night. Eventually she opened herself to a different way of interacting with music other than dancing. She began to play the flute.

When doubt enters into our spiritual lives, we can express it, explore it, and surround it with love. It is important to acknowledge it like Teresa of Calcutta. Her long dark night lasted most of her ministry. It didn't stop her. She persisted in her love of others and in her prayers. This is what we can do. Persist.

Reflection Questions

1. When have you felt abandoned by God?
2. What "why" questions do you have for God?
3. What might help you persist in the face of doubt?

Ease to Fit

He heals the brokenhearted, and binds up their wounds.

—*Psalm 147:3*

There are books on finishing techniques for knitters. Even if you can knit like a pro, the garment can look "homemade" if it's not blocked and sewn together well. Panic sets in when I read the words "ease to fit." This means that one side is longer than the other and yet the knitter is being instructed to sew the two sides together. For me, easing to fit requires a lot of time and pins as I try to cajole the long side and short side together. Easing can create puckers. The idea is to make the puckers as small as possible and evenly spaced.

Easing doesn't mean to force fit. Easing requires patience, time, and finesse. It's about taking two dimensions—two pieces of flat fabric—and turning them into a three-dimensional sweater.

Our spiritual lives are about taking our different experiences and integrating them so that we can become a self-differentiated person. This is challenging when we experience something difficult like a loss, a betrayal, or something unwelcome and unexpected. Healing is the way to ease our way back. It's God's love that pins us back together, that helps us fit back into our lives, that forges a seam between two incongruent sides.

The seam never fits perfectly together. Even the best knitters have trouble making two pieces that are different shapes lay perfectly flat. Healing doesn't mean we don't have scars. The scars are a reminder of our past. We learn to take the experience and use it to find out more about ourselves. What was my part in the relationship? How can I change? What do I want to do differently in the future? What do I want for my future?

Fitting a difficult or challenging experience into the fabric of our lives requires asking the right questions. What aspects of our lives do we control? We can't change others. We have to knit our lives with the materials we have in the best possible way. We are in charge of our patterns. Sometimes we have to stretch our short sides to ease to fit, to incorporate the pattern of others. Sometimes we have to tear out and reknit sections even though the original stitches have put their marks in the yarn and made it less pliable. But with God's help, we can heal and we can ease to fit.

Reflection Questions

1. What piece of my life do I need to ease to fit?
2. What still needs healing?
3. How can I reframe (reknit) my experience?

CHAPTER FOURTEEN
KNITTING WITH MUSIC

Contemplative prayer is conducted in silence. We try to quiet our minds and embrace the presence of God, but there are times when the thoughts become too loud. Our inner voices won't settle down, and we are plagued with one thought after another. Even if we are successful at letting go of these thoughts, they keep coming like leaves and sticks floating on a river after a raging windstorm. We can't find the depths of the river among the debris. Our minds churn, and the debris collects in the eddies. Music can clear the debris. Music can slow the raging river of thoughts and provide a life raft.

Dolores, a hospice chaplain, created a playlist of "Amazing Grace" by every artist she could find. She found fifty different versions. This playlist grounded her every time she felt discouraged or anxious. The words were the same, the melody was the same, but the expressions were vastly different. Dolores encourages her patients to be creative in their music selections. "Find music that can take you places," she suggests. "Listen to hymns, spirituals, classical music, chants, choir anthems, contemporary Christian music, or whatever else brings you closer to God. You'll know it when you hear it," she says, and her patients agree. After some experimentation, they find the right music that moves them into another world, a place of peace and beauty.

Knitting to music activates another sense. We feel the yarn, we see the colorful stitches, and now we hear the music. The

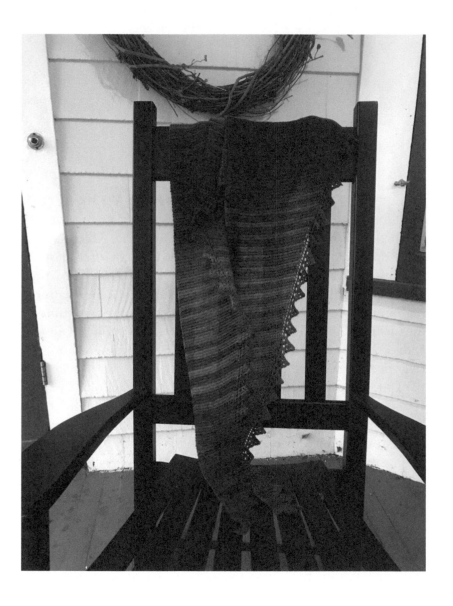

tiny movements we make with our hands become our dance, a way of feeling the notes in our bodies and connecting with the sound viscerally. Music can quiet the mind and help push away distracting thoughts and anxieties that prevent us from being aware of the presence of God. Instead of trying to will away the thoughts, we can allow the sound of the music to displace them. Our focus is centered on listening, feeling, and seeing. As our thoughts diminish, we can gradually decrease the volume until we work our way back to silence.

Sandy loves hymns, and she has a list of hymns for each liturgical season. She immerses herself in the seasonal hymns starting with Advent. During the long season of Pentecost, she experiments with a variety of sacred music, trying new genres and composers that sometimes startle her senses. Sandy describes music as the energy that fuels her prayers, grounds her in time and space, and helps her keep her priorities in order. Sacred music is the soundtrack of her life. She listens to other musical genres, but she finds listening to sacred music throughout her day is what allows her to sink into the contemplative silence when she sits to knit. She is already in a place of peace.

Experimenting with music is a way to pull ourselves back to our spiritual practice. Music can bring energy when there is none, when we feel depleted or discouraged. It can be a salve for our grief. It can underscore our joy. It is a gift.

Finding the right music to support our spiritual practices is a worthwhile endeavor. We can start by googling ideas, asking friends, listening to sacred music stations, following our favorite composers, artists, and choirs. Sometimes the music finds us. We hear a song on the radio or a hymn in church, or maybe a melody comes into our head.

Carol found herself humming a tune she didn't recognize. When she was visiting her mother in the nursing home and absent mindedly humming the tune, her mom asked her why she was humming the tune to the song "Sentimental Journey." It was a very old song that Doris Day, Ella Fitzgerald, and a number of other artists sang starting in the early forties. "Your father used to sing that song all the time," Carol's mother said. "Are you thinking about your dad?" Carol realized that she hadn't had a chance to grieve for her father because her mother had a stroke the week after her father died. Music brought him back to her. She chose to sit with the music and experience the loss. Every day when she sat down to knit, she would play the song a few times and then settle into her contemplative silence.

Once we have decided what we want to listen to, we can find a quiet place, gather up our spiritual knitting, and let the music wash over us. Music can bring us back to a place where we are able to enter the silence of contemplative prayer. It can calm the mind, displace the frenetic thought patterns that we experience, and help lead us back to silence. When it seems impossible to sit in quiet, we can use our knitting and music as a way back or as a way to give expression to our feelings.

1. What music inspires you?
2. What music fills you with joy?
3. What music helps you with grief?
4. What type of music do you find the most healing?

Take Time to Reflect

Making Connections through Prayer

Let the same mind be in you that was in Christ Jesus.

—*Philippians 2:5*

People often ask me how prayer works. This is a difficult question. What I know is what I observe from my own experience. I sit in prayer and usually nothing happens. Sometimes, an idea will come to me, but mostly it's just a nice comfortable silence. I sit and knit, praying the Jesus prayer "Lord Jesus Christ have mercy on me" in rhythm with my knitting needles. It used to be so much harder; my mind would just gallop from thought to thought. My spiritual director used to say, "You can't help the thoughts that come into your head, they are like birds landing on tree branches, but you don't have to let them build a nest." This wonderful image enabled me to shoo the thoughts away or write them down if they are important.

Prayer is a time to be open to God. We are like stitches about to be cabled. We make room for God by moving our usual thoughts aside just like we move stitches from the main needle onto the cable needle. Now we can prioritize our time with God. We knit God's stitches before we knit our own. When we become part of the pattern, we find our stitches intertwined with God's stitches and something beautiful emerges. Prayer creates new patterns, and we begin to find that ideas come easier, relationships improve, there is a deeper awareness of God's presence, and everything seems different. Prayer helps us align ourselves with God's will and allows us to see the moments of grace that happen all around us.

I worked part time at a small inner-city church. Our music program needed to change, but we didn't have much money and we weren't sure exactly what we wanted. Both Cindy, the rector and I put this problem in our prayers. We asked God for help in discerning what would be best for our small but devoted congregation. Our Sunday worship was the fuel that energized our volunteers that worked in our city gardens and our weekly food pantry.

A guest singer and piano player, Kyle, came to the church and played at the wedding for his brother, one of our parishioners. We loved the music. It was inspiring, and we both thought this style of music would inspire our congregation. We wanted to hire Kyle until we found out his current salary. There was no way we could afford a musician like Kyle.

We kept praying.

We decided to post a job description for a musician with Kyle's skills. People started applying, but either they wanted too much money or they didn't have the skills. We were disappointed but we kept praying.

Then a letter arrived in the mail. "Dear Cindy and Julie, I'm very interested in being part of a mission-orientated church like yours." It was from Andy, a young man just twenty-four years old who was playing piano and singing at a church thirty miles away. We asked him to interview.

Andy's music brought us to tears. His voice was strong and clear, his fingers graced the keys with a gentle touch, and he truly believed what he was singing. He only lived two miles from the church and was commuting thirty miles every Sunday to play. He believed in our mission and he was excited to play for us. Here was an answer to a prayer, a gift from God, but how could we make it work? His current church was paying him more than we could hope to pay.

He needed a location for his piano studio and we had the perfect spot. Thank God we did not give up on our prayer. Here was the perfect solution for both of us. He could have a piano studio rent-free as part of his package. His piano students brought new people into the church every day. It all worked out.

Our prayers had linked us to Andy. Our separate stitches intertwined, and we were knitting together the community with his musical gifts. Regular prayer provides us with the courage to persist even when what we are trying to do seems impossible. It helps us unite our will with God's will to create the best possible world, and like the best knitted cable pattern, the stitches twist and turn around one another forming one beautiful pattern.

Reflection Questions

1. What have you observed about your prayer life?
2. Has prayer helped you persist through difficult times?
3. What would change in your life if you had the same mind as Christ?

CHAPTER FIFTEEN
EVANGELISM

The best evangelism happens through words and action. A knitting friend of mine decided to share her faith one Lent by presenting a challenge to the knitting community. Mary Ellen had felt a call in her prayer life to take action. She summoned all her knitting friends to help her knit forty shawls in forty days. She wanted to have forty prayer shawls to bless on Easter Sunday. As part of this challenge, she set up times for knitters to gather at local coffee shops to work on the shawls. The word spread, and knitters seemed eager to make this project their Lenten discipline. Mary Ellen ended up with more than forty shawls. On Easter Sunday they made an impressive sight draped over the altar rail. There was a multicolored hand-dyed shawl in the shape of a triangle, a rectangular shawl in brown tweed, a round white lace weight shawl, and dozens of others in all colors, shapes, and yarn. The shawls were the visible prayers of the knitters. The sanctuary had become a gallery of their Lenten reflections, conversations, hopes, and desires knit into each stitch.

The project did more than just produce beautiful shawls, it brought together a community of knitters who wanted to dedicate themselves to giving love and comfort to others. Their gatherings gave them a chance to share their faith, their Lenten experience, and their sense of call from God. It was a safe place for knitters to support and encourage one another on their spiritual journeys. Some knitters came to knit but went home with

invitations to experience a church community. The relationships that knitters developed participating in the group made it easy to offer a personal invitation to church.

I like to ask people how they came to be part of their church community. Everyone has a story and although the stories may differ, they usually involve one person asking another person to come with them to church. It is the personal invitation that makes the difference. Steve had become acquainted with Sam at one of the shawl-knitting groups. He noticed how well Sam seemed to be coping with his recent job loss and asked him why he was able to be so calm. Sam replied that he was supported by his church community and their support gave him the strength to keep going. He explained that he was so grateful to be a part of this particular church family and then he invited Steve to church. Steve accepted and the next week reported back to the group how welcomed he felt. Steve said it was like coming home, and he was even encouraged to knit on his Lenten shawl during the service.

Knitters have an immediate connection with each other through their passion for knitting. Get a few knitters together and they will be laughing and talking in a matter of minutes. The first step of evangelism is about forming relationships. As we get to know one another, we can create opportunities to share what's most important in our lives.

I carry my knitting with me wherever I go. When I knit in public or with other knitters, I get out the prayer piece and place it in front of me. Then I take out the project I want to work on and start knitting. Knitters will ask me about the work in progress that I have taken out of my bag. Why bring it out of the bag if I'm not going to work on it? I explain that this is my prayer time knitting, which leads to more questions, and soon we are talking about God, prayer, following Jesus, church, and our own spiritual histories. I find that knitters are happy to have someone listen to their spiritual stories and are interested in how knitting can help them deepen their relationship with God. As the conversation winds down, I put forth an invitation. Sometimes I invite them to my church, sometimes I offer suggestions of other church homes that might work for them, and sometimes I offer to pray for their spiritual journey. There is always an offer of support and encouragement.

Spiritual knitters can be catalysts. The forty shawls in forty days is one way to spark conversation and to invite people into a work of mission and ministry. There are other ways knitting can be used as an evangelism tool. One church's knitting group hosts "Quiet Days for Knitters." They open their sanctuary one Saturday a month for knitters to come and knit in silence. For knitters who want to knit and talk, they open up the fellowship room. The church offers a child care program so mothers can bring their babies and toddlers.

Joyce brings her six-month-old daughter and her three-year-old son every month. She lives for these times of knitting peace and quiet. Joyce shares the child care with twelve other mothers so they only need to volunteer for child care every six months. Joyce told me that her time in the sanctuary connects her with a feeling of deep peace. Sitting among the stained glass windows in the quiet helps her reconnect with God. For this time, she is free of the demands of the twenty-four hours a day, seven days a week of child care. A knitter from the parish invited her to church. After a few months Joyce went and then joined the church. Now Joyce is actively reaching out to other young mothers to join her.

Many people today have not experienced what it is like to be part of a healthy church community. Their experience of church is either nonexistent or not helpful. They may have been forced to go to church by their parents and required to participate when they didn't fully understand the church's teaching. Others were not raised in any religious tradition and have no idea where to start with the rituals and unfamiliar language.

Knitting circles are a way to invite people who are grappling with theological questions to explore Christianity. One Christian knitting group publicizes in advance the theological question they will be discussing each week at their group. They invite content experts as guests to guide the conversations. They had a youth minister speak about children and their images of God. They hosted a church history professor who spoke about the role of women in the church. Their discussions are lively and the group keeps creating lists of intriguing topics to maintain interest. Two knitters from this group, Virginia and Kati, find the conversations riveting. Neither one of them have ever attended church, but they both have lots of questions. Kati said that this group has given her insights into Christianity that have changed her perceptions about the bible. Her curiosity had grown to the point where she decided to attend church on Sunday.

Evangelism is about creating relationships of trust where stories can be told, treasured, and shared. It is about helping others become aware of God's presence in their lives and to hear the call to help create the kingdom of God on earth as it is in heaven. A church community enables members to discover their own unique gifts and talents.

Virginia used her organizational skills to overhaul how volunteers sign up for missions at her church. In the process she met more people and became more invested in how her church was reaching out and helping single mothers in the inner city. The new mothers they encountered were young and overwhelmed. Virginia enlisted Kati and a few more of their friends, and they started knitting ornate baby sweaters in multiple colors. These tiny sweaters were miniature works of art and came with an invitation to join the new mother support group at the church.

Knitting is an excellent way to build relationships and a sense of community. A knitting group or a knitting project brings people together and provides a less intimidating door into the church community. People who have limited experience of church rarely show up on a Sunday morning without an invitation, and the invitation has to come with enough information to spark their interest. This takes time. Knitting together and telling stories can create the kind of relationships that might be open to an invitation to join the community on a Sunday. Many churches have a knitting group already. It's easy to invite people to the knitting group. It's the first step of knitting evangelism. Evangelism is about giving the gift of a loving community to others.

Take Time to Reflect

Save Yourself

Acquire the Spirit of Peace and a thousand souls around you will be saved.

—Seraphim of Sarov

Seraphim of Sarov, a famous Russian saint, uttered these words back at the end of the eighteenth century. My spiritual advisor paraphrased the quotation this way, "Save yourself and thousands around you will be saved." Saving yourself means acquiring the spirit of peace freely given to us by God. Acquisition starts when we pray because prayer is saying yes to God. When we become aware of the grace that God gives us, we naturally want to respond. Grace transforms us into different people. We tend to forgive rather than nurse a grudge, we feel thankful instead of irritable, and we are able to show our love to others more easily. When we are changed, our response changes those around us.

Georgia, a friend of mine, was recently blessed with twin grandsons. The love and joy she experiences as a grandmother enrich her already full life. Georgia is the knitter I talked about earlier in the book. She knits socks for people. She has made so many, she could knit them in her sleep. Each time she has to wait, she pulls a pair out of her bag and knits. The sound of the clatter of her needles and the rhythmic pull of the thread from her bag is calming. The countless socks she has knit through the years have been given to family, friends, and complete strangers who may be mourning a loss or just received a cancer diagnosis. Even as a new grandmother, she kept knitting, and the new babies became used to the sight of their grandmother with needles, yarn, and a growing sock in her hands.

I saw Georgia at our Diocesan Convention recently. Georgia showed me two pictures. The first picture showed her two-year-old grandson pulling on a pair of socks that Georgia had knit for him. As parents and grandparents know, it is quite a feat for a two year old to put on socks. Usually they are tight and hard for little fingers to open and pull over their toes. Not Georgia's socks. They were perfectly made for her grandson, who joyfully was able to do it himself. The next picture was her grandson frowning intently at the knitting he was holding in his hands. Is he knitting? Not yet, but by the expression on his face, he is captivated by the miracle he has seen happening since the day he was born. Save yourself, acquire the spirit of peace, and thousands around you will want it too.

Reflection Questions

1. How does your prayer life affect the people in your life?
2. What does Spirit of Peace mean to you?
3. How do you feel when you are with someone with an active prayer life?